Made to Fail

13 secrets of successful start-ups

Matthew Cain

First published in United Kingdom in 2013

ISBN-10: 1475289537

About the author

Matthew Cain had a successful career ahead of him before he launched Newscounter – a right to reply website. He then got lucky and co-founded Trufflenet, a social media research business. Matthew is a fellow of the Royal Society of the Arts through which he helps early-stage start-ups. He is a Trustee of Cardboard Citizens.

About Enabling Enterprise

All of the proceeds from the sale of the book will be donated to Enabling Enterprise, a social enterprise founded by Tom Ravenscroft, a Teach First graduate. Enabling Enterprise's education programmes help teachers by integrating enterprises skills development into different areas of the curriculum for all school-aged children.

Acknowledgements

This book would not have been possible without the encouragement and advice of my diligent, enthusiastic and patient editor Lisa Carden, Matthew Taylor's comments on various drafts and advice on publishing from Sian Edwards and Kevin Duncan, thanks to introductions from Phil Jones. Without Tom Ball the creative genius of the Trufflenet brand would not have existed – and this book would be called 'How not to be a successful start-up'. But particularly to the intrepid entrepreneurs who opened up and shared their stories: Alistair, Andi, Becky, Bibi, Isabel, James, Matt and Perry. Their stories make this book worth reading.

And I couldn't have written the book without the opportunity to start Newscounter. For that I owe a huge debt to Matthew Taylor for introducing me to the idea and Nigel Clarke, the Newscounter board and investors for their support in pursuing the project (and then Trufflenet) long after many others would have lost confidence. To them and the staff at Trufflenet I'm forever indebted. They, and friends such as John Murray, lost money despite their incredible and generous contributions. Trufflenet's clients invested in the business in a different way and I'm grateful to their courage for supporting a start-up. This book is an attempt to show all of you what I learnt thanks to your courage.

And finally my children and parents may not have had a choice in the matter but my wife most certainly did. And she persisted where lesser people would have walked away.

It should go without saying: all mistakes are mine alone.

Table of Contents

Introduction

There's a right way to start a business...and there's the way that *I* started a business. Neither is guaranteed to work. But do it my way and there's a high chance of failing big. My first start-up was called Newscounter. It failed. I failed. But what separates the failing start-up and the successful start-up is simple. One generates cash quickly, at low cost. The other doesn't. It's a simple distinction. Easy to write, hard to achieve. So how do you find the winning formula? Because every entrepreneur begins believing they are going to succeed – and most then fail. Maybe you've either got it or you haven't: that elusive combination of skill, charisma and daring-do. Maybe it's just chance: you just happen to have an idea that people really like – and which you can make and sell for the right price. Or maybe it's experience: you have to have experience of setting up a business that doesn't work to learn what it takes to be successful. That's certainly what a lot of people write in business books.

But none of these are satisfactory explanations. If it was all down to personality then successful entrepreneurs wouldn't fail.

Yet they do. If it was all about chance then entrepreneurship would be the only discipline known to man which couldn't be enhanced by learning. And if it was just about experience then no first-time entrepreneur would ever be likely to succeed.

I thought I knew the answer. As Newscounter failed, we found customers for a new idea. All I had to do was make it and we would have a successful business. And it didn't turn out like that. It wasn't just about the right idea. So why was the start-up recipe so elusive? I found four successful first-time entrepreneurs and studied them to see what they had in common. Without knowing it, they'd all stumbled upon the formula for success. They happened to start the business the right way. It was an accident of circumstance, not a product of design. They didn't develop their businesses according to the rule book.

There's a theory from the United States which advocates many of the core features we found in the successful start-ups – the 'Lean Start-Up' principles. But strictly applied, they make sense mostly for companies specialising in software development. And those that invest most time in discussing start-up models theories tend to be distinct from those most likely to start a business.

Starting a business *is* risky but it doesn't have to be suicidal. Risks can be measured and proportionate.

The right person, taking the right risks, has a better chance of success. It might not be where you thought – it might not even be what you expected, in fact – but by focussing on the core tasks, you are more likely to succeed at something.

So this is not just a book. It's a campaign to spread the word. To help people thinking about starting a business to do it in the right way. To show them what's possible. To discourage them.

To point them in the right direction. Thank you for supporting that campaign. It's a worthy cause.

Chapter one

How I screwed up my start-up in four simple steps

1. A winning idea

Have you ever had an idea that was so beguiling that immediately you had to abandon everything to pursue it? No, me neither. This story begins when I fell in with the wrong crowd. I met them whilst at university. It's a common path for self-destruction. It just usually involves more substance abuse and less business plan abuse.

It was the dawn of the new millennium. I was working in a think-tank, hearing endless conversations end with a whinge about public debate. If only people knew the real story, these earnest academics opined. Politicians should step in and regulate newspapers. Like that would ever happen.

My boss had a better idea. Matthew Taylor had previously worked as the Labour Party's 'Director of Rebuttal', the PR version of a counter-attack. When it worked, the counter-attack would turn the news on its head. The story would change from 'Tories accuse Labour' to 'Labour attacks Tory claims'. Journalists reported the row, whilst the original assertion got lost in the detail.

Imagine that happening on a website, he thought. It wouldn't take hours, but just minutes to change the news. It wouldn't be dependent on organisations persuading journalists to shift the emphasis of a report. You could reach the public directly and the accused would have the right of reply. The truth would have its boots on before a lie ran around the world. I thought it was an interesting idea, but unlikely to work in practice. I couldn't imagine it would be particularly interesting for the website's readers or achieve very much for organisations.

Two years on, I was working in a PR agency. 4 August 2004: one particularly tough hangover; unshaven; yesterday's shirt. Not a good start to a new business meeting. Nigel Clarke, a client with a problem. I turned to my old boss for help – Matthew. We needed to catch up anyway. It turned out he was still plugging his 'right of reply idea'. I could help. We'd call it Newscounter.

His argument was powerful. Trust in journalists was low and each day there were lots of sensational newspaper headlines based on wild claims and half-truths. People were turning from newspapers to the web for their news. The public wanted transparency, not more spin.

The web offered the opportunity to 'disintermediate' – to remove the story-tellers and allow the public to judge competing arguments for themselves.

Matthew's website would publish allegations, inviting users to vote and demand that the accused reply. Their response would be published in full and in their own words. Readers could then judge which side of the story was more persuasive. If the accused chose not to exercise their right of reply, in the face of considerable public demand, the absence would tell its own story. The website's users' votes would provide a new angle on the story. Real-time polling would put public opinion at the heart of the news.

It could be a charity. Matthew had been working with a number of people in the voluntary sector who shared an interest in encouraging more informed media debate. Many people were supportive. A not-for-profit organisation would receive grants and donations. It would probably be seen as impartial and fair.

A charitable model could be difficult, though. There were concerns that the Charity Commission could be nervous about something that would, at times, be seen as political. Besides, the pitch to corporates would be complicated as a charity.

Would your call be diverted to the wrong department? Would a business fear that it would be tapped up for a donation? And would large donations from wealthy, anonymous donors undermine the perception of objectivity?

I wanted to help Matthew. It would be good experience. And I thought there was money to be made. A commercial website could reach an even larger audience and do more good. The running costs would be low and the minimal staff time spent on administering the service. The main cost would be the profile, and the importance of that would decrease over time as people became more aware of it. If it would be a business then Nigel Clarke might be interested. As a former PR chief executive he had valuable experience. Now we had a great idea and the necessary experience. We just needed to prove it.

A business would be professional. Transactions would be simple. We'd make a phone call to an organisation in trouble; a simple pitch – they'd already have heard of us, probably. We'd take some money from them, copy and paste their statement onto our website, wait for our users to vote on whether their response was more persuasive than the allegation and then move on to work with the next customer. Transparent, self-interested, straightforward.

I started with the supply. I was thrilled to find so many stories in which the headline in a national newspaper contained a strident allegation would contain only a single sentence, right at the end of the article, from the person or organisation in the firing line. Sometimes they didn't even get that.

The longer I spent with the idea, the more I liked it. There were plenty of potential customers: government departments, local authorities, football clubs, the BBC and numerous celebrities. I just didn't know who would want it most, first. So the website would need to encompass a whole range of topics – current affairs, entertainment and celebrity scandals, sport and science – to be flexible to demand. That spread would also mean it was interesting to the largest possible audience. Potential customers would leap off the pages of the national newspapers each day. Most of these had advisors – PR agencies mostly – and organisations had press offices dedicated to responding to journalists. They would be the people who would decide to use the service. But would they want to?

2.   Writing a Business Plan

Demand would be high once there was demand for the service. That statement really is as facile as it appears. Customers would use the service when lots of people visited the website.

That would give them high exposure and awareness of their response. That was worth paying for. But people would be drawn to the website when they could use it to call powerful newspapers and organisations to account. For that to work, it needed to be a popular website with lots of customers. How to build that cycle?

Marketing, and particularly PR, would be the answer. Matthew's media profile was critical. He was a frequent media commentator and pundit throughout his career. His departure from government would raise eyebrows and offer a new stream of insights for journalists. That would get us over the first hurdle, and a board of high-profile directors would also help.

So actually, in its first phase, the website wouldn't need tons of visitors; just enough of the right kind. Customers would be attracted to use the service because it would get their response directly to journalists and opinion-formers, we felt.

More interest would be generated by the content on the website. It would provide new angles on the stories of the day. The BBC could report that newspapers had over-reached themselves on a story. Lunchtime news bulletins would report '*Daily Mail* under fire for misleading Tesco article' whilst evening news programmes would move on to (say)

 'Tesco under fire as shoppers reject its response to tax allegations'. The business could create the news on its own! We had no idea what to charge, though. I reckoned that £500 per job didn't sound like a lot. The fee was negligible compared to the cost of taking legal action against inaccurate news stories. It would be faster and more public than a complaint to the (then) Press Complaints Commission and preferable to finding yourself in a crisis. The fee was equivalent to a couple of hours' time for a mid-ranking PR advisor. Even if the business got only two customers a week, at that price it would be a profitable operation. And surely I could get that?

The fee wasn't important, we decided. Organisations would do anything to buy their way out of a crisis. There were large communications budgets and some companies and private individuals found money for legal advice in a crisis. We were providing another tool for the experts.

It would be exciting. We would be the darlings of the industry, making and shaping the news. We'd be media commentators, reviewing the papers, pundits on the TV, the place to go for a fresh perspective. There'd be consultancy, conferences and cocktail parties. We'd finish work late and roll into Soho House. Web start-ups were fashionable. We'd be at events alongside Google. We'd license the idea globally.

Finding a solution to inaccurate media coverage would be like fixing the weather. I wasn't sure that I would be a millionaire before I turned 30. But I *could* settle for changing media debate in the UK.

3. Raising money

All of this we knew. The task to write it in a business plan was tedious. The business would have two big initial costs: building the website and salaries. The website needed to look good to give people confidence that it was a serious endeavour. It needed to allow the public voting so that people understood that it was impartial. And we'd need fulltime staff to run the service. It would be nice to raise £250,000 but we could make do with £100,000.

We started working out the income we would need to raise the start-up capital. We would need to be in profit early in year two and worth £1m at the end of the third year. It didn't seem fanciful. We would need to grow from two customers a month (to break even) to two customers a day (to justify a £1m valuation). We could grow more through either price increases or expansion into other countries. This wasn't challenging. Just an effort to make a case to investors.

I spent some time wondering why no one was already doing it. I assumed that PR agencies lacked incentive to innovate, and that the industry was so competitive others would boycott a service backed by another. There were plenty of technology entrepreneurs but this idea needed an editorial oversight which couldn't be automated. Newscounter couldn't scale infinitely, so perhaps tech experts were put off. Or maybe they didn't like the idea of appearing on the 'Today' programme. There weren't many people who had Matthew's understanding of rebuttal who would also be willing to take a risk on a new venture, but there weren't any significant barriers to prevent either group from setting up a right to reply service. But mostly I was pleased they weren't and keen to ensure they couldn't.

That made me protective of the business. It became a jealously guarded secret. There was little intellectual property in the idea and we certainly didn't have an 'invention', but we also knew that securing some IP would make the business more attractive to investors. We tried and failed to find and file a patent, so settled with a trademark. I remember the adrenaline rush (or possibly just panic) when similar ventures were reported in the press. I also had a frustration at the media stories that would have benefited from our service.

I felt keenly that we could have helped, that we'd missed a chance to establish the value of our service.

We needed to speak to potential customers. But we had to be careful. Not too many, and only the right sort. I didn't want to embarrass Matthew by making his involvement more widely known. Prospective investors were presented with a non-disclosure agreement (NDA). We focussed on high-level, well-networked people. I didn't want to talk to anyone who would be underwhelmed by the idea because they lacked the vision to understand it as it. And we couldn't talk to anyone who would be so overwhelmed that they might try to mimic the idea.

We had few conversations with trusted individuals, including an audience with the founder and chairman of a PR agency that represented most of the FTSE100. He told us about other services that enabled companies to communicate directly with key audiences. We thought it interesting yet irrelevant. He made no firm commitment, but none was sought. We weren't particularly discouraged; you'd expect someone like that to be cautious.

As soon as he saw what it did he'd want to be involved, we told each other. There wasn't much more we could do, we assumed. Without a product to offer, we couldn't elicit firm commitments.

Without a product to demonstrate, we couldn't expect to either.

I ran the idea past a senior colleague who had provided the start-up capital for a number of marketing services businesses. I thought he'd be excited by the networking potential. He asked me if we'd got anyone signed up. I explained, as patiently as I could, that we didn't expect anyone to sign until we could show them how it worked. He asked to be kept informed.

An established, wealthy healthcare entrepreneur met us and quizzed us on the business plan. He said that we'd end up making money in a different way. We weren't on some expedition. We just wanted to set up our business – this business. I assumed he hadn't been listening when we ran through the exhaustive list of ways in which we could monetise the website – advertising, conferences, and expert advice. And if we altered the plan to fit each investor's advice we'd have had as many plans as prospective investors. It may have got us investment, but it wasn't developing the business.

A year on and we'd met a few investors. I knew we hadn't got beyond first base, but not why. I didn't know what second base looked like.

We could keep going, but we weren't getting anywhere. We just needed to make progress, and that meant getting the costs down.

4. Making the product

I phoned a friend. He could build the website and was persuaded to take equity equivalent to his time. If we cut the marketing costs down to nothing, we could run the business for a year with less than £50,000. Nigel said he would take care of the money. I spoke to the designers at work. They could produce the website design. It would be expensive to us, but I knew their print design work was excellent. They gave us only one design option – but that was all we could afford with our £5,000.

By May, it was clear that Matthew wasn't going to be on board after all. He'd taken another job running a large organisation. The business would be down to me – or it would not happen at all. I had to do it, surely? My friend was building the website. I'd got Nigel involved. It was too good an idea to go to waste.

It would be nice to just get going, to set up a blog. But the site needed to cover multiple issues a day. I couldn't do that in my spare time – it needed to be well-networked. I couldn't call PR agencies from my desk in a competing PR agency.

The media profile would mean I would need to keep leaving the office. Besides, the website needed the vote buttons to generate the media interest, which required an expensive web build.

Yes, Matthew's profile had been critical to building demand. The marketing and PR budgets had felt very important. But this was the web. We could make it happen if we had a great idea. The idea deserved to have its day.

So it might not work, but not trying would be even worse.

Starting badly makes failure harder

Monday 2 October 2006: Newscounter's first day, giving the right to reply to a grateful nation. Nigel was now the principal investor, Matthew a director, me the receptionist, office junior, account director and CEO. We were about to change the world.

The doorbell rings at 2am. The newspapers have arrived. I read every article on every page to find stories in which the organisations weren't given a right of reply. I write a short summary of each story and publish it on the website. Back to bed by 5am. Up again at 8. Then – nothing. No calls. No visits to the website. At 9am, I email the public relations departments of each organisation featured in the stories on our site with a brief introduction. Nothing. At 11am, Karen looks at the website. At 3pm, I buy the *Evening Standard* to identify a new set of stories. The day deflates. We knew it was going to be hard. Now we'd learnt just how hard.

On day three, the first rebuttal. It's massive. It's from Liverpool FC. The institution I can depend on when all else fails. My eternal love.

I've phoned and spoken to the press office. They actually say they'll send me a statement.

The website gets some hits from a link I've posted on a fans' forum. They vote to demand the club reply, before someone removes it for being commercial spam. Then the reply arrives. No, no money changes hands, but that's not the point. We knew it would take time.

By the end of week one, we'd had the first 1,000 website hits. Maybe it was progress.

Slow to change

Matthew suggested we organise a small breakfast for a number of people who might be interested in the idea. We gathered together the founder of MySociety, which setup successful citizen web services, some colleagues from PR agencies and a couple of journalists. Matthew opened the session explaining that we'd set this thing up and we'd like to know what they thought and how we could develop. I was perplexed. We didn't *need* ideas. We had the idea. We just needed supporters. They just needed to back us. Talk about us. USE THE SERVICE.

We showed the website to the group and the reception was lukewarm. One person even suggested we give up now and join forces with a charity operating in a related field. Not the sort of tactful help we needed. It was probably Matthew's introduction that confused them. It had been too broad, when what needed was focus.

Hours later, there was a call from *Press Gazette*. I wasn't ready for it. Nervous, I babbled and said something about Newscounter being quicker than the ineffectual Press Complaints Commission. The article appeared with a dismissive response from the PCC. It could have been worse. But the article hadn't got across the power and potential of our idea. Perhaps the journalist was too defensive and thought it was an attack on the profession. We needed to be more careful: with so few friends, we couldn't afford to make enemies. But these were green shoots. Unpredictable, uncoordinated – but maybe that was just how these things worked.

Several weeks later, Matthew checked in. We were holding steady at 1,000 website visits a week, and one or two organisations replying per week. He's talked about the website to a renowned PR networker who had set up a business which initially appeared as an alternative solution to our problem: a forum for PRs and journalists to gain more shared perspectives. She had looked at the site. The design was terrible, she said. It wasn't clear who it was for or why they would use it.

My face reddened. I opened the website and as I heard the words, the scales fell from my eyes. I felt naked. The embarrassment. Matthew suggested we pull down the site and replace it with a blog, pending a redesign. That was too much, surely? We didn't have any money for a redesign. A blog would look amateur. We were *a business*. And what about our 1,000 readers, not to mention the investors? We mustn't frighten the money. I just couldn't admit defeat.

We needed to develop the service. We decided to find other websites interested in the same stories as us. We'd post a link to our site inviting them to vote for a reply. We'd then come back and post the reply on their site and suggest they judge whether it was persuasive. That would boost traffic and the more votes, the more persuasive our pitch. We might even get enough traffic to generate advertising revenue.

I couldn't do it alone, though, so we found our first member of staff. She was a former journalist and had the perfect skills: she was used to pounding the phones, getting replies from press offices. She could work mornings from home. It would save the cost of an office. She might even be able to do the odd early shift. It would free up my time for networking.

December came and we were getting nowhere. We were now spending £3,000 a month. Stories came and stories went, and each day became a huge effort just to save face. Nigel's questions become more persistent: has anyone paid for it? I was confused. I thought he understood.
We were still focusing on generating interest, surely? We couldn't expect to charge anyone yet.

But the money was running out. Not in some heroic kamikaze fashion but the most gentle asphyxiation. If we had vanished overnight, no one would have noticed. But then it would all have been for nothing: all the money would have been lost but nothing better would have come along in our place. I had to keep going, fixing the problems we'd identified and continuing to build awareness. Eventually customers would come. We always knew it would take time. But it wasn't clear what time would achieve. But failing to maintain the service would guarantee that we lost momentum. What would have been left? And what would I have had to do?

There's founder optimism. But this was foolishness on a grand scale. I was failing to interpret the feedback that was on offer. We weren't in a hole – it was a well. The aching tiredness that was caused by 03.30 starts, 7 days a week, removed from me the very capacity to think and plan that the business so desperately needed.

I didn't continue because it was rational. I didn't continue because I was stupid. I continued because I couldn't see an alternative. The daily process was comforting; a cloak of hard work hiding the nakedness of failure.

If I had actually just made a chart of the website hits and the number of rebuttals per day, it was painfully obvious that there was no momentum – just a series of occasional twitches on a dead line.

Changing, not earning

The New Year brought new resolve. We had to do that website redesign. Until then, we couldn't really expect anyone to pay for the service. We would need a proper launch, an event at which people could hear from Matthew why Newscounter was such a good idea. That would persuade them and generate some press interest. We would get a blog on the website to provide some commentary and make a professional pitch to clients. We went back to investors to raise more money. We'd learnt so much during our soft-launch phase. Now we'd give the business some proper momentum. That would cost money. But these things just do to do well, we assumed. Clearly I couldn't do it all alone. There was just too much to do. And we needed expert intervention.

We found a PR agency to work for us and developed the product further, giving customers an evaluation report. We also promised some free search engine advertising so that people looking for the news story would see that it was in dispute.

Then after using the service, we would send the client an evaluation report showing how many people saw the story, where and what they thought of it.

That felt more professional. It was now a proper service for managing online reputation, rather than a strange hybrid between advertising and PR.

In May 2007, we launched the redesigned the website after raising more money from the investors. A new look and a high profile; we had something to shout about. It was a second chance. We'd fix the flaws and rescue the dream. This had to be front page news for *PR Week* and surely more important than the usual stories about a mid-ranking PR executive moving from one large WPP agency to another.

We prepared to make the best possible impression. Every angle was considered. The Groucho Club was booked for a breakfast briefing. It gave the right image – and we couldn't afford other popular venues. We checked the date didn't clash with other major events. I was given some formal presentation training. A designer produced some branded PowerPoint slides. We printed a branded

Newscounter folder which could hold loose-leaf pages and a business card. Five pages were written to explain the service, what it did and who we were. We even had two case studies – although no actual endorsements. Invitations were sent to the top figures in the industry.

We survived the pre-launch hiccups: my computer crashing the night before, the back-up failing, the website crashing two hours before the launch. The building works outside the Groucho meant I had to strain my voice, but half of the expected attendees came, no one left early and the website held up. Maybe this would give it the shove it needed.

I'd imagined collapsing after the event, spending the day drinking champagne. Instead it was back to work to get some activity on the website. And to receive the resignation of my team member. The journalist fancied a career change. Well, the day was always going to be memorable.

Not knowing when to quit

Two days later. *PR Week* is published and our launch appears as a small story on page seven.

It was enough to elicit an unsolicited call from a FTSE100 company. Ok, so the size of the story was frustrating. But it worked. There are some signs of progress – more free rebuttals, more website hits – but still no income.

The Department of Health became interested.

They'd use Newscounter for free but they said we could meet afterwards to find out whether we could work together. That would give us the opportunity to sell – or at least understand what we had to do to get them to become a customer. By our estimates, they needed our service twice a week on average.

We carried the story and implemented the reputation management service. A week later, I sent the evaluation and some dates for a meeting. Four weeks later, they tired of my phone calls and emailed to say that they wouldn't meet. It just wasn't that interesting. We were learning it wasn't working, but not why.

Tesco used the service. A TV documentary had raised concerns about food hygiene. It was fantastic to be working for one of the

best and biggest corporations in the country.
Their digital response was already well
executed but perhaps they thought we could
plug some gaps. At last, this was our chance
of commercial success and I could prove I
was entrepreneurial. I found the email
addresses for the relevant people in other
supermarkets. (Not a moment to lose, was my
thinking.) I sent a case study around the
industry. Tesco called. I had been
unprofessional. They were not endorsing our
service and would not deal with us again.

July came and it was dead. I was just going
through the motions every day, trying to keep
things afloat in case we got lucky. But there
was no hope, never mind expectation. I just
had to do something to fill my time. The days
dragged on. There was nowhere to go,
nothing to do. It wasn't my decision to pull
the plug on the business. But I needed
another job. But how would I find one?

In August, summer doubt had transformed
into despair. Google enabled users to add
comments beneath search results. If there was
any need for a right to reply, Google provided
the means – and the audience. What were we

going to do? The game was up. I remember confirming the news with the chairman. We couldn't go on spending the money. No one protested.

Two strokes of luck arrived almost simultaneously. We stumbled across a new idea. And completely coincidentally a potential customer came to us and asked us to develop the very same product. It was a second chance,

A real business. I couldn't see how I fitted in – I didn't bring any of the necessary skills – but I owed it to the board to take it as far as I could. That business would become Trufflenet. It wasn't an overnight success and I still got plenty wrong, but we built a business. More of that, later.

I wrote this book because every year, tens of thousands of people start a business in the wrong way. They find out that what they did doesn't work. Then that's it: a dream, an ambition, family savings – all wasted. They don't have the chance to put it right. And they've often followed chronically poor advice. But you don't have to get it wrong to get it right. You *can* know how to start a business before failing.

Why failing isn't a step to success

Is there anything we could have done to make Newscounter successful? The question was enough to slowly drive me mad. But I needed to know why. Not just as a way of making sense of the last three years, but also to know what to put right as we created Trufflenet to monitor consumer comments on the web. We'd done so little right, it was hard to know where to start.

The first website design wasn't good, but the second was. But neither attracted enough visitors. The pitch to the first customers was too complex. It became simpler and customers understood. We got organisations exercising their right to reply. They just didn't want to pay for it. Maybe there just wasn't enough public interest in the website. Maybe we'd learnt more about how to run a news website than we'd learnt about how to run a business.

We had never actually become a business. Plain-talking folks would say that

Newscounter failed because it didn't sell enough (any) product to enough (any) customers at the right price. Simple. But expensive management consultants would also have plenty to say. We didn't identify the right fit for the product with the market. Awareness in key customer segments was insufficient to generate returns. The business wasn't optimised for scale. The business didn't leverage its potential public profile sufficiently to generate income. Complicated, but not less right.

We thought we had put right the biggest mistakes when we started Trufflenet. This was an idea that had a customer waiting. We showed them how it would look and what it would do. They thought it would meet their needs. Again it would need a significant amount of start-up capital to build the IT system – but the case to investors would be more compelling.

But we also knew that having a good idea wasn't enough. We had to get customers' attention. We had to give them what they wanted. And Newscounter must have had some valuable lessons for how we should develop Trufflenet.

The idea

Perhaps Newscounter hadn't been a good enough idea. Nine out of ten people we spoke to liked it, but it didn't elicit strong emotions. There were too many 'ifs'. It would be valuable for organisations but work only *if* the website had lots of users. The website would have lots of users only *if* it had unique content from organisations.

Both would be attracted to the website *if* it created rows which were reported in the media. Rows would take place only *if* the public and organisations used the website. You could see how it could work – but not how it could get there. And even if it did, the benefits to users were not quantifiable. Yes, it was cheap. But there was no evidence of value.

Trufflenet wasn't just an innovative idea. It was a solution to a new and emerging problem. Companies were beginning to face criticism online directly from consumers. There were websites emerging to help organise and stimulate customer complaints. We already knew that one company, my kitchen supplier, had not taken a proportionate approach to solving the customer complaint. Trufflenet could create a compelling customer case for investment, demonstrating actual costs arising from a failure to handle complaints properly.

It was not an exciting idea but it had clear commercial potential. It wasn't going to change the world. It might not even make it a better place. But businesses needed the service and would be grateful for it. Even if I was slightly disappointed.

Business model

Newscounter has been underpinned by an unreliable business model. We would never have been able to predict each day's customers. There would be no certain revenues at the start of each day. The pitch was 'buy now'. Tomorrow wouldn't do. And for most organisations, they'd be buying once. We thought it might be easier to sell to an organisation in a crisis, but couldn't prove it.

We thought the urgency of the situation could work either way, and proved it didn't.

Trufflenet had a much more predictable business model. Clients would subscribe to the service on an annual basis. Fees would be charged every 30 days. The costs of additional clients would be marginal, once the software had been developed. The main cost would be adding storage to the system as client numbers increased, but that was relatively insignificant and a cost secured against revenue.

Business plan

There had been too many things in the Newscounter business plan of which I had a general understanding but lacked specific, detailed knowledge. The weakest part of the plan was the market research.

We hadn't methodically approached potential customers to find out what they thought of the product. We were too worried about keeping it secret. We had no idea of the overall size of the market and had done no serious competitor analysis because we had no competitors.

Newscounter wasn't scaleable in the same way as Trufflenet either. It would always have needed people at the core of the business identifying stories, editing the website and promoting the content. Yes, it was a service business which could be replicated in other countries, but even the underlying code would need to be re-purposed to work in other languages.

Newscounter raised a relatively small sum which we had been planned to be spent slowly through the year. We had less than £40,000. Maybe that just wasn't enough to launch a business. Even if I had not taken a salary, the money saved wouldn't have achieved very much.

Trufflenet had a more methodical business plan. We replaced guesses with knowledge. The PR agency tested various different costs with its clients. We learnt that we could charge £3,000 per month rather than the £5,000 we had originally guessed, but even then we needed fewer than 10 clients to break even.

The PR agency represented six major potential clients and there were 30 other agencies which were larger than it and between us we knew someone in most of those agencies. So we had a reasonable expectation of getting to meet some key gatekeepers, even if they weren't decision makers. If the short term looked good, the long term looked better. If clients signed up via a website, the opportunity for global expansion was already built into the business.

This business truly was scaleable. Each additional client would be a marginal cost. Having clients on long-term contracts meant that we knew how much we could invest in marketing. Analytics from the website would help us evaluate the marketing more effectively. And even if we couldn't generate a single press story, we didn't need to do that to get straight to customers.

We started to discover competitors and at first that was alarming. I hadn't expected that. None was apparent on search engines, but then I wasn't sure what people were looking for. And it was clear they weren't doing a particularly good job. Lots of companies hadn't begun to consider monitoring the web. But some competition showed that there was demand for the software. It gave us other companies to learn from.

Trufflenet needed to raise money. A lot. We had to find a business that could develop the IT and we also needed to pay for the design of the system, the product name, the marketing and a new website. Even if we could persuade some people to take equity, we would need the best part of £100,000. And by now, with a child on the way, I would need a proper salary. That couldn't be in dispute.

So the stakes were higher, but the upside clear. We now had a solid business and a solid business plan. Not the sort of day by day narrative but a business model and set of projections that would ensure we would make a success of the business.

The product

The design of the Newscounter website was the earliest problem we were confronted with. We had designed it without consulting potential customers and it became immediately apparent that we couldn't generate significant interest in a website with such a poor design. We fixed the design and increased the number of users voting on the website. We had some better comments from potential customers. We would have to get the design of Trufflenet right first time.

Maybe the Newscounter product hadn't been well delivered. Perhaps if there had been video it would have been more compelling. Maybe if we hadn't been so prescriptive in our neutrality we could have explained the story more, been more forthright. Perhaps if we had the skills to build website, we could have made more changes more quickly.

Customers wouldn't have anything they could 'touch' or 'see'. It was a service but one without clear benefit. If you bought it, what would you be getting? Even if there had been a larger audience for the website, how many users would have been 'enough' – 1,000, 10,000 or 1 million? We just didn't know.

Trufflenet was much more obvious. We knew *precisely* what the product needed to do – and therefore what it needed to look like. And when we showed that to the PR agency, they didn't dispute the approach. It had to be instantaneous. There was no point telling a company about something that had been hurting its brand for months. The software had to give you access to content quickly. It had to tell you whether it was good or bad. It had to tell you whether it was important – if it had lots of readers or very few. What the customer did in response would be up to them.

The important insight for Trufflenet was its ability to tell a client whether the content was important. That was the value that would have saved my kitchen company its compensation. To do that we needed research to develop an algorithm. I read how Google had done it and experimented with different equations. As long as we didn't under-rate the importance of something, we would be ok in the short term. It could become more sophisticated with time. That would become our USP, raising the barrier to entry to competitors.

Provided we did not miss content, the product could clearly 'work'. Clients would see how frequently the search was being performed and how much data was being identified. That would clearly demonstrate value. If it found nothing that they needed to know about, it would be an insurance policy against things going wrong. Clients would rather know that there was nothing to worry about than just assume.

So product design, functionality and customer benefits were all clear. The fundamental issues with Newscounter would be fixed by Trufflenet from day one. We weren't going to get *that* wrong again.

Skills

I set up Newscounter because no one else would. If I hadn't volunteered to run the business, it would not have been created. Or even worse, someone else might have done it. My USP was my willingness to do anything, and my low cost. Ok, so I might not be a particularly good salesman. I understood PR but I wasn't going to be invited onto TV shows. I could edit the website, although others might be able to do it better. But I could do everything just well enough to keep things going until we could employ experts.

Having failed so miserably, I was convinced that I added no value to Trufflenet. I understood the web and why people were using it, but that was useful and interesting rather than valuable. I wasn't an IT developer and didn't understand the area in enough detail to be able to manage the development of the software. Once it was complete, I was fairly certain I wouldn't make a particularly good job of selling it. I would try, and try my best,

but I didn't expect any great returns. We would certainly need to hire good people to run the business.

Conclusion

I was convinced we were on to a good thing with Trufflenet. It wasn't just the power of self-persuasion. We had evidence to support it. A PR agency waiting to buy the software. A powerful story, evidence, that the software was valuable. And a clear product which met our imaginary client's needs: it found content quickly, comprehensively and understood whether it mattered.

We had discovered why Newscounter didn't work and we'd put that right from the start with Trufflenet. It would be a proper business. Now we had got a failure out of the way, we could get on with making a successful start-up.

Right?

The difference between knowing what's wrong and knowing what's right

Trufflenet's path to success wasn't as smooth as we'd expected. No, really. It started so well, so differently from Newscounter. I knew what I needed to put right. We started with a customer, a PR agency. We knew the problem our software needed to fix – so we knew what the product needed to do. We found a software developer who would work for equity (we didn't have the cash) and worked closely with a good designer to produce the product that the customer would use. We produced marketing materials ready for when the software was completed. We would hit the ground running.

After some development hitches, Trufflenet began trading in November 2009. We started well: customers began to fall into our lap without us doing very much but that meant I didn't know what to do. Sure enough, three months later, progress had slowed down. Two customers walked away and a third never signed up. A fog of uncertainty fell. They had been convinced by the sales pitch. It did what we told them it did. But something was going wrong. Maybe we needed to show them the value of what we *had* found.

But how could we if it hadn't caused them reputational damage? Could we place a value on absence?

There was more uncertainty about how we secured new clients. The website wasn't bringing leads but we didn't have a budget for producing marketing material. We did some free analysis for companies in the news – but that didn't pique their interest. We appeared to have landed customers by luck, which wasn't repeatable. Different people in different organisations with different job titles had bought the service so we couldn't draw any lessons from them. No one baulked at the price – but that may have made it too cheap.

Trufflenet was now costing over £10,000 a month and the pressure was on. We needed activity – but weren't clear what. We needed to generate sales – but from where? We needed satisfied customers – but weren't clear how. We knew that the software wasn't quite meeting customers' expectations – but not why. The product was right. The marketing was right. The business model was right, even if I had missed the targets. The idea couldn't change. So what on earth was wrong?

We redesigned the dashboard and got some expert advice on how to do it. The end result was much, much better. And made no impact on sales. Another chunk of money had been spent without return.

Luck saved us, again. A PR agency commissioned a study to 'listen to' online conversations about haircare. We provided them the data six weeks later and they turned it into a beautiful book, presenting the different themes and topics with topline ideas for a strategy. That was it – a clear benefit for customers. It wasn't a piece of software that required time and investment but instead genuine insight into consumer opinions presented in a visually attractive but dependable way. Soon we were simply prospective clients reports that we'd produced for other businesses, and they could then choose what they wanted.

We produced proposals setting out questions we would answer and reports answering those questions. We had a repeatable model.

By October 2010, 11 months in, we had a business: a growing set of clients from a known segment of the market; a clear understanding of our competitors; a well-rehearsed argument about the benefits of our approach compared to theirs; an understanding of what our customers valued and what they didn't. And we also had a clear path showing how we could add more value. It wasn't the business we had expected. But we were too pleased to ask why.

We had made a new set of mistakes, however. We'd started the business with a lot of money. Bought expensive software that didn't quite match our customers' expectations. Spent lots of money on marketing that didn't achieve very much. Chased income without a clear understanding of why. And we'd been left without much money to correct our mistakes.

Were these unavoidable mistakes – things we had to do as part of the process of getting it right in the end? Were we just victims of circumstance? Had Newscounter not taught us enough? There was a nagging doubt that once again, we'd started a business the wrong way. That it wasn't about fixing the marketing, getting the price right, writing a good business plan – or any of the other things that I thought I'd got wrong with Newscounter. Perhaps my entire approach to setting up a business was wrong.

Why business books are wrong

No one pretends it is easy to start and build a successful business. Many pretend the answers are somehow mystical. There's a group of best-selling authors who claim that they've found the secret ingredient, and that ingredient is usually... themselves. A unique blend of personality, attitude, skills and experience.

You too could be like Richard Branson if you were like Richard Branson.

There is also no shortage of 'how to' books. These suggest that setting up a business is a process. You research the market, write a business plan. You identify the risks, the competition and the opportunities. You write this all down, tick the boxes and create your business. Whether you are making jam from your kitchen or manufacturing widgets in Asia, it's all about the process. Many successful businesses do this, but so do many failures.

For others the answer is experience. Entrepreneurs can expect to fail, and are most likely to fail early in their careers. Many successful businesspeople have followed that path. So all you need to do is get on and start your first business. The faster you do it, the sooner you'll learn what you are doing wrong. Then you'll be able to move on to the next opportunity so that you can get it right. There's wisdom and insight in these books.

But what if you don't fancy failing? What if you can't afford to?

Some books record the unique set of skills used by superstar entrepreneurs. It's about the strength of your network, about good time management. About being passionate, yet disciplined.

Having a relentless capacity for hard work and a narrow vision of what you're trying to achieve. These books aren't wrong. But they aren't useful. There are plenty of people who exhibit all of these traits. Many are entrepreneurs, but many others are failed gamblers. They are neither unique to entrepreneurship nor to success.

As discussed earlier, the technology start-up movement, particularly in the US, has developed the concept of a 'lean start-up' – originally articulated by Eric Reiss. The core idea is that you launch a business in the same way as you do software. Launch early – when you have a 'minimum viable product' – and then test and iterate until it is fit for purpose. In America, there is a mini-industry devoted to this model of start-up businesses alone. It works very well in software. But other businesses need start-up costs. Whole industries are ill-suited to a model of constant iteration. A restaurant cannot become a hair salon overnight.

So much of the business book canon left me mystified. I knew that what I did was wrong, but not all mistakes matter. And some helped lead us away from the failure of Newscounter to the relative success of Trufflenet. So how do you distinguish between the three sorts of mistakes?

Management consultants have a three-part model of error:

1. skills-based errors where the actions made were not intended;

2. rule-based errors where the actions match intentions but were not correctly applied;

3. knowledge-based errors where the actions are futile because they are based on incomplete knowledge.

I had without doubt made all three kinds of error. But which type mattered? Skills-based errors are transparent and fixable. You can work on a skill and achieve incremental improvement. Rules-based errors can be corrected because you can see that the action is not having the desired effect. It requires you to challenge your assumptions – but that's essential for entrepreneurship.

Knowledge-based errors are insidious. You don't know what you don't know. Everything that you do know appears to be in order, though, so you plough on. You challenge mistakes and correct assumptions, but the mistakes that you miss can end up leading to failure.

Errors of knowledge are the most frustrating. Why didn't I know? How could I have learnt? It's also alarming.

The successful start-ups I studied for this book avoided knowledge-based errors by circumstance rather than design. That means thousands of businesses fail because entrepreneurs lack fundamental knowledge about the optimum way to start a business. That's market failure.

I had to discover what it took to build a successful start-up, for the first time. Could businesses make money in the first year? Were they all just tremendously risky? Were the founders just more skilful than me? Or had I learnt the wrong lessons from Newscounter?

How smart start-ups succeed

I needed to find out how entrepreneurs could be successful with their first venture. I needed to speak to businesses that were sufficiently new that they remembered the early days, but they'd been in business for long enough to show that they're not a flash in the pan. Entrepreneurs who didn't have a public image that they needed to protect. I wanted to find people who didn't have lots of personal wealth because that wouldn't provide a template for others to follow.

It wasn't enough to know that it is possible to develop a business in your spare time with very little money. That's obviously much easier if you are an IT programmer selling things over the internet. But does that model apply to businesses that need start-up capital? How can you operate with minimal costs if you need a shop front? And how do you get a product to customers quickly if you are operating in a regulated environment? To identify lessons that were useful to all entrepreneurs they had to apply to different sectors facing different hurdles to starting a business.

I found four businesses that met these criteria. I studied their accounts.

I spoke to their customers and their peers. And I interviewed them. It confounded everything I expected.

These people did not get the knowledge they needed from a book. They didn't get it from a business advisor. But for different reasons they started their businesses in a way that maximised their chances of income without increasing the risk of failure.

What do they have in common? Superficially, very little. The founding entrepreneurs have very different backgrounds, skills, work experience and education. Their personality types are as different as their products. Their businesses needed varying levels of start-up capital. Their ownership models vary. But they are all making money – and a fair amount – within months of starting-up.

They all started their businesses in the same way, however. On day one, they all had a product that they'd sold. They could identify their first and second customer. They knew the price they should charge. And they hadn't, and didn't need, to spend very much to get in front of customers. They were the polar opposite of Newscounter. Here are their stories.

Bim's Kitchen: Putting the product before the business

Civil servants don't understand business. They aren't entrepreneurial. They can't take a risk. The civil service is about strict hierarchies and the organisation obsessed by processes. Civil servants have a comfortable existence, certain not just of the salary at the end of the month but training, career enhancements, decent holidays and a nice pension. These views are widely held, and held deeply by many of their political masters.

Civil servants do make unlikely entrepreneurs. But it was the civil service that made Bim's Kitchen. It was the perfect start-up, because, rather than despite the fact that it was unplanned. And it was all because James shared his lunch.

James Adedeji – Bim to his friends – learnt to cook as a teenager living in Nigeria. Despite being an ambitious and successful civil servant, he knew that he wanted to do something associated with cooking at some point in his life. And he always knew it would be called Bim's Kitchen. James and his wife, Nicola, had toyed with the idea of running a bed and breakfast. James was clear he didn't fancy the monotony of working in a restaurant. But he did have a clear critique of African cooking in Britain. He knew the sort of restaurants where he could eat African cuisine. And where he wouldn't take his white British friends.

It isn't clear that James ever wanted to be an entrepreneur, but he did want to cook. We all know someone like James: talented and passionate about what they do but with those skills firmly locked into a hobby whilst a career pays the mortgage. The civil servant in James hasn't gone completely. He remains a cautious, thoughtful man. He is comfortable with analysing detail and assessing options. James isn't obviously impatient but life runs to James' timetable. Our meeting started late, and finished later. His wife's efforts to dodge the traffic wardens of Hackney were admirable. But his mind-set meant that James wasn't ready to start a business – although he already had.

Getting a decent sandwich in Whitehall, where James worked in the Department of Health, is a challenge, so he avoided it and brought his own lunch to work instead. Inspired by his cooking lessons in Africa, this was a world away from his colleagues' cheese and tomato on sliced white. And sharing food was part of James' culinary culture.

And that's how Bim's Kitchen started. James liked to share his lunch, talking to colleagues about what he made.

He spent time working in a minister's private office which is perhaps more collegiate than some parts of the civil service. James liked cooking sauces and talking to colleagues about the sauces he made. As word of mouth spread, he found himself selling sauces at the end of meetings. And there are a lot of meetings in the civil service. James was making £200 a week, cooking late into the evening after work and developing his relationships with colleagues. In fact, his jars of sauce already had a label, produced at home to announce Bim's Kitchen. Then one day a colleague was heading off to visit family in Hong Kong to ask for a bulk order. James thought it a casual request initially. That the next time he was making some, his colleagues would like a few extra jars. He'd misunderstood. It was a serious order for around a dozen jars. As word spread, more orders from other paying colleagues followed.

At roughly the same time, the department opened a round of voluntary redundancies. James surprised his colleagues by applying and made clear to the decision makers that it was a serious application. Bim's Kitchen was about to become a full-time enterprise.

There was no business plan. No start-up costs and no company mission statement. No patents were filed, no spreadsheet was troubled with a cash-flow forecast.

James was just keen to get his sauces to more people. It was easier for him to decide on the price for his product than it is for many start-up businesses. There's a clear range on offer at a supermarket. And customers expect to pay a premium at a food market. (In fact, charging too little can go down badly in places like North London.) But the market has established an expectation. A jar had to cost less than £10.

James and his wife opened a stall at the farmer's market near their house in Palmers Green, selling five different flavours of sauce. He'd make as much sauce as he had time for and stay on the stall until it was sold. The Bolognese sauce remained the best-seller, as it had been in the department. Word continued to spread and James took a stall at two other London food markets – Borough and Alexandra Palace. By now, weekends were consumed by sauce: on Saturdays, James would work at Broadway Market whilst Nicola was at Borough Market, and on Sundays James would be at Alexandra Palace and Nicola at Palmers Green.

James is talkative and engaging. He loves his cooking. He likes watching how people react to the different tastes. He wants to introduce people to African cooking. But if he has a favourite sauce, he won't say. There's no hint of regret about the sauces that haven't made it to the market stall.

He is relaxed and easy-going. Optimistic, but not evangelical. On the stall, he doesn't push forward his sauces or talk you into tasting one. There's no hint of the global footprint that now lies behind the business. He seems as surprised as he is pleased about that good things have happened to his business. But there's no pretence or showmanship. Let him talk for long enough and you could be persuaded that it's all to his wife's credit. If you could stop her telling you how clever *he* was.

James' cooking sauces were good ones that people liked to eat. And cooking sauces were popular: a step-up from ready meals without the hassle of starting from scratch. Another chef/entrepreneur, Levi Roots, had made waves on the BBC's 'Dragons' Den' with his range. Making cooking sauces is smart because it scales: each sauce weighs a couple of hundred grams and so many jars can be made from a single domestic cooker. But they are still another range of cooking sauces. They may have been scarce amongst the stalls or organic farm produce of London food markets but supermarket shelves are groaning under the weight of sauces made by multinational firms from Sharwoods to Parmalat. James may have been earning money from a hobby but it wasn't clear that there was much room for growth.

James thought hard about what he was cooking and why. He spent time in supermarket aisles, learning from the competition. He spoke to customers about what they did with his sauces and what they liked most. And James spent a long time talking to his wife about what they were doing and why. It wasn't just that James wanted to cook. It wasn't particularly that James wanted to make cooking sauces. He wanted to bring the ingredients, flavours and style of *African* cooking to more people. James wanted it to have the same wider acceptance as other regional flavours, such as those from India, China and Thailand, had gained years earlier.

It turned out that James was capable of the 'cool calculation' so beloved of the business world, even if it cannot be found in his demeanour or on his CV. Bim's Kitchen would be 'inspired by Africa'. It would focus entirely on African fusion cooking. Bim's Kitchen had a clear mission and identity.

They'd found a USP. And so James took the riskiest and bravest decision of his business career to date: he dropped his best-selling Bolognese sauce. In its place, and inspired by a customer suggestion, James, went on to develop what has now become their biggest selling product- their African Chilli Coconut Relish. James continued to share his food casually. But now it was clear what he was offering.

There was an audience for fusion cooking. He'd remembered a trip to Rick Stein's restaurant in Cornwall and Stein's interest in this type of cuisine. James found contact details for the store manager of Rick Stein's shop in Padstow. He sent some samples. James wanted to know whether he liked them. Rick Stein and the manager not only liked them but wanted to stock them, and that's when Bim's Kitchen grew up. The first jars of sauces were going to be sold from a retail shelf beyond the family.

Moving from marketplace to shelf brought with it various regulatory compliance issues. Without complying with the relevant legislation, James wouldn't get the deal with

Stein's stores and they'd never get to break out from the small independent food markets. This was a cost but not a risk – there was a stockist waiting, and one who shared their vision. Bim's Kitchen didn't need to pay for expensive advice or consultancy. The store manager helped James understand the legal requirements for labelling, and other requirements like determining the product shelf-life: the tests that produce the 'best before end...' stamp you see on all food.

The core attributes of Bim's Kitchen remained. The sauces were still cooked in his kitchen.

The ingredients would now need to be measured properly but the labels were still designed by James and printed on his home PC. Packing them into boxes and shipping them remained a family affair.

James also wrote to Peter Gordon, a New Zealand TV chef who is famous for pioneering fusion cooking. James had long admired his work and wanted feedback. You can guess what happened next. Gordon not only gave long, detailed feedback about James' sauces but also provided an endorsement that James could use in his marketing. Months later, James received an enquiry from a food store in the United Arab Emirates. Peter Gordon had visited and they'd asked him for advice on where to source the food that he recommended. He put them in touch with Bim's Kitchen. It was now an international business.

New sauces were introduced as James experimented with more ingredients and the business continued to grow. There were deals with independent retailers in London and beyond. Word of mouth brought enquiries from the most unexpected places: Bim's sauces were inspiring African cooking in Wales, the Lake District and the Midlands. There was a tentative inquiry from a supermarket which James rebuffed.

The financials were tempting but it would have meant handing over the recipe to a commercial kitchen. James wasn't ready to lose control over how the sauces were made.

But now there were more jars sold by strangers than by James and Nicola. He could no longer look each customer in the eye as they reacted to the taster pots. They needed to develop their brand. Social media, and particularly Facebook, gave them an opportunity to reach customers directly. The business could test new ideas with a couple of hundred of its biggest fans. And it provided a means of getting repeat custom from the casual customers who encountered them on a market stall.

Food awards continue to help build Bim's brand: the sauces have now won several Guild of Fine Food "Great Taste Awards". And with pop-up markets the latest fashion in London, there are plenty of ways for the family to spend their weekends. And during the week James and Nicola look after the suppliers – and the cooking.

It remains a business with very few fixed costs. The accounts are kept by Nicola's father, a retired accountant, and there are no employees to manage. There is insurance to arrange and inspections from food hygiene authorities to manage but these early costs could be met by the income from the market stalls. There was a basic website, banners for the market stalls and a small branded van. On every stall they opened taster pots for the sauces to be spread on crackers. But once a prospect had tasted the sauce, served to them by a family member, there was a high conversion to customers. Everything else went into the cost of producing the sauces. The jars, the labels, the ingredients were all bought to order. As long as James didn't go wild and make many more jars than he could sell, the business would be secure.

With one exception: salaries. James and Nicola can live frugally. But their mortgage – not to mention their children's Christmas presents – depend on the business. Working out the value of their contribution to the business is hard. James had the redundancy settlement from the Department of Health. And he remains, at least in part, the careful, cautious civil servant. And it hasn't harmed the business but helped it thrive.

James did everything possible to reduce risk from starting his own business, but of course it wasn't risk-free. Without regulatory compliance, he wouldn't have been able to sell to anyone other than friends and trusted colleagues. And market stalls alone weren't enough. If James hadn't quit his job at some point, he and Nicola wouldn't have been able to make enough sauce to live. Without interest from stockists, they wouldn't have been able to reach enough customers to have a viable business. And his insistence on cooking the sauces himself guarantees quality but also runs the risk that a bad batch will be costly at best; at worst, it could fatally damage the brand.

It was so simple for James to start the business I need to remind myself how tough it can be for others. Anyone could do what James did. There must be thousands of people who are good enough cooks that they can make sauce that strangers would like to buy. The market for sauces may be massive but so is the competition. The genius is the African inspiration. James' personal story may not be unique but Uncle Ben's spends millions of pounds trying to replicate that authenticity in its TV commercials. James built it through a brand designed on his home PC. Visually, it amounts to little more than a common or garden typeface and a map of Africa. But it works.

The business continues to grow. Since our meeting James has sold 2,400 jars to American giant TJX, which runs the TJ Maxx and Homegoods stores across the US. The deal was secured after a buyer spotted them in a British shop last year. The sauces passed a taste test and the buyer tracked down James and Nicola to secure the order.

The company has already exceeded its targets for 2013 and, all being well, will shortly face an exciting challenge of how it increases production.

Bim's Kitchen created a market within a market – demand for African cooking sauces. James developed an authentic brand without cost and continues to run a business without waste. All the while, word continues to spread of a message created without consultants or marketers and fashioned out of the decision to ditch his Bolognese best-seller. It isn't a million pound business yet but it's making a profit and on a clear path to growth. It's a successful start-up in a competitive market.

Key points

- James made excellent sauces and he knew people wanted to buy them.

- He proved he could sell sauces *before* Bim's Kitchen became a full-time affair.

- Little money was spent – and none wasted – on marketing, branding or communications.

- The business learnt from its customers but wasn't afraid to drop its best-seller to create a clearer proposition.

- James knew how to expand the business beyond a hobby.

Blue Tit: Understanding your personal and business interests collide

How do you make a success on the high street? It always fascinated me because there's so little room for experimentation. It's what I'd got so wrong at Newscounter. I thought running a business was like running a shop. You set it up to sell something, you told people. They came or they didn't, they bought or they didn't and you'd succeed or fail. Then along came the sirens of Silicon Valley with their 'lean start-up' principles. That's all well and good, but not if you are on the high street. But plenty of are successful. Indeed, they represent a particular British success story.

To the untrained eye, high street shops aren't innovative. They sell what customers buy. It's a way to make a living but it's not particularly innovative. They don't find new markets. Some locations work, others appear perennially unsuccessful. Luck seemed to be a big part of it.

That's why Blue Tit was such an allure. It didn't conform to any of the start-up lessons I learned. And it was hard to see how it could.

It was a high street hairdresser's. There are certain things it needed in order to do business.

A shop, bowls and showers, mirrors, lights – and hairdressers. You could cut corners but you still needed to cut hair. And if people didn't want their hair cut there, you couldn't pivot to become an off-licence.

So how do you minimise the risk for a start-up? Start with location. Blue Tit might be a business studies dream. There's an old question: where do you put an ice cream van on a beachfront? In the middle, of course, to maximise potential custom. So where do you put the second? Half way to the left or half way to the right to have the best access to the remaining sunseekers? No, next to the first.

And so Blue Tit is a hair salon in Dalston (Hackney, East London) next to a hair salon. In fact, it isn't just next to one hair salon. There are five within 50 paces of each other. But it isn't just 10% cheaper, 10% better or with marginally more attractive stylists. Blue Tit is innovative, even transformative.

The typical price of a haircut on that stretch of road is £10. For that, you get a quick and efficient session with an electric razor. Blue Tit charges men £35 and women even more. That's what you'd pay in a central London salon, a Toni & Guy or other salon aimed at young professionals with an eye on style. The local salon owners in Dalston laughed at Blue Tit.

They didn't mind *that* sort of competition. They said you could charge those prices in their neck of the woods.

Blue Tit was fully booked in its first month. In its second, it hired more stylists. It posted a profit and opened a second salon within the first year. There was no competition from the other salons. They'd found a totally new market. In fact, sometimes they can be found sharing haircutting tips with their neighbours. The Blue Tit team enjoyed learning how to braid, even if it wasn't immediately useful.

So what business genius lay behind Blue Tit? None. Not in a traditional sense, anyway. Blue Tit was created by two friends, Andi (Andreas Hinteregger) and Perry (Piotr Patraszewski), with no prior business experience. They are too trendy to be businessmen. So much so that Andi has to remind himself to 'think like a businessman' he says. They embody the relaxed 'vibe' that they wanted to create for their salon. There are other Shoreditch salons like theirs, they say, but they are a bit pretentious. People go there to be seen; they're 'try hard' venues.

It's tempting to assume there's nothing 'try hard' about Blue Tit. Success certainly seems to have fallen into Andi and Perry's laps.

I live nearby and noticed the store evolving as it was fitted out before launch. With bare brick walls, comfy chairs and a counter, it was easy to assume that it would be yet another bar in Dalston. Once complete it still looked like a bar, but the anticipation had been enough for me to mention it to a neighbour who said it would be a hairdressing salon. It was enough to get me in through the door in its first month. The apparent popularity of the place helped, too.

Opening until 9pm Monday to Saturday (with a shorter day on Sundays), the shop usually appeared busy and vibrant. The table and chairs outside created a community feel. I returned each month to a business with new stylists but an apparent consistency of quality. Nothing seemed to go wrong. By May 2012, they were confident of opening a new salon in Clapton, on the edge of the Olympic Park and the 'next big thing' in the spread of trendy hipsters through East London. By summer 2013 the third salon had opened in Peckham, south London.

Timing was important. The first salon arrived within six months of the opening of Dalston Superstore, the popular bar which put Dalston on the map. It brought in a new, young crowd to the area and, thanks to the expanded Tube line, increased property prices and mobility in the area.

Business might have grown more slowly if they'd launched a year earlier. A year later and there may have been another salon vying for customers – although most new retail businesses in the area are bars and cafes.

I assumed that Andi and Perry were riding on the wave of the property market. They must have picked Dalston because they knew where it was heading. I had visions of them leaving a warehouse party and deciding to set up a business on the street. In fact, the decision was more pragmatic. They knew they wanted to be in the area but couldn't afford Shoreditch.

Andi and Perry decided to go into business within moments of meeting each other. They shared a vision for the style of salon they wanted to run and a similar outlook on life. There was no business plan and no market research. But they knew how to make cash last.

They got a good deal on the rent and the first three months free. Without this, they were prepared to walk away. Andi says that if they'd tried to open the salon nine months later, the rent would have been too high. The way they tell the story, it is free of significant emotional investment. It's a fun project – perhaps like a full-time hobby. But they want to build the business they work in. It wasn't about the area, the salon, the name or even a career choice.

So Blue Tit may not have been a Silicon Valley-style garage start-up, but it was as lean a business as it could afford to be. They did the entire shop-fitting themselves, often working through the night to get the salon ready for launch. It took a couple of months after the lease was secured. Andi felt it was a long time.

There were no trimmings of the customer experience, but no money wasted either. On my first visit, the gowns were not branded and no plastic protectors were placed on my shoulder. There were no hair-sweepers or bored receptionists. There wasn't yet a website. In fact, I hadn't experienced it at its most lean. Such was their need to launch quickly, the phone line hadn't even been installed when the doors opened.

They started the business with their life savings and contributions from family. In total, roughly £20,000 covered the lease, the utilities and the cost of materials for the salon.

Despite the parsimonious approach, customers didn't suffer. The drinks were free and included generous helpings of beer, wine or smoothies, depending on your preference. The walls may have been bare but were creatively so.

The furniture had been rescued from a vintage store – and looked stylish for it. The footstools were simple, tatty wooden things but entirely in keeping with the culture of the salon.

Andi and Perry are fantastic hairdressers. Their cuts are consistently good. They have that marvellous knack of making all male cuts lasting an hour which gives the customer a sense that care is being taken whilst ensuring that later customers are not kept waiting. Whatever happened at Blue Tit, they could earn a decent living from cutting hair. They are able to spot these qualities in other people. As Blue Tit has hired more stylists there has been no obvious decrease in the quality of haircut.

The business could have just made a profit if Andy and Perry alone had been operating at near capacity. But it would not have grown. They would not have had the time to keep the salon clean, to ensure that the appointments diary was kept well or that new projects, such as the website, were delivered efficiently.

Significantly Andi and Perry had no expectation of getting rich from the business in the near future. They began the business with enough savings to last about six months. They live a frugal life. The few hours they are not working, they are asleep. Neither has mortgages and their rents are low. They continue to take as small a wage as possible. And at the end of the year, the profits are reinvested into the business. Andi particularly dislikes the idea of paying Corporation Tax.

Their outlook has given the business the best possible chance of growing. If they had expected to earn a fair wage in the first few months, they wouldn't have been able to hire more staff and customers would have found somewhere else to get their haircut at short notice. Now it means that they can expand the size and scope of each salon every year. It's a simple equation: they either take the money themselves to reward their hard work or take a risk on becoming wealthier in years to come.

When you've decided to put money into the business rather than your own pocket it makes you particularly careful with the business' cash. When Andi tells of a costly mistake, you can see a real frustration that the money was wasted. It may have only been £5,000 – a small amount even for in the first year of Blue Tit – but Andi is pained to have lost it.

Andi and Perry have a similar view of risk to Alistair Crane, the CEO of Grapple and another case study in this book. They genuinely feel they had little to lose. Andi says that he could have lost his savings and then would have worked for someone else. Other people are that phlegmatic when they lose a dry cleaning ticket.

So if you can't start a hair salon in your garage, what else can you do to maximise the chance of success? By building customer relationships from your front room. Andi and Perry had a number of private customers that they'd served in the months before launching Blue Tit, and balanced these against other jobs. When the salon launched, they were confident that there would be a base number of customers even before new ones were attracted to the newly opened shop.

And they knew it was going to work within weeks of opening. The salon was fully booked in the first week and for most of the first month. Andi knew then that it was commercially viable. He'd worked previously for a salon at start-up stage, so knew what it would take. He understood what proportion of customers could be expected to return and roughly how often. From that base, they had enough to sustain the salon in Dalston before they'd run out of money (personally and professionally).

But they learnt the right lessons from the location of the Dalston salon. Clapton was starting to draw in residents who could no longer afford to rent in Dalston. And there was an emerging number of trendy bars and restaurants – although not on the scale of Dalston. And Peckham's path to gentrification was different again. The Blue Tit founders learnt the right lessons from Dalston – and confirmed their model in Clapton. A combination of low rent, vibrant street and a growing population of young, stylish residents with a decent disposable income.

It's not just about cutting hair. Andi and Perry want to do business in the right way. For them, this has meant a counter-intuitive approach to marketing. They haven't really done it. They aren't really comfortable with some of the obvious ways of building customer loyalty. It would conflict with their vision for the salon experience. Pushy stylists working on commission and over-sold products would create the wrong 'vibe'.

In fact, the salon has done very little marketing ever. The website is not advertised. Clients are invited by text to the opening of the new salon. A brief period of PR was scrapped after not generating results. There are no flyers and neither is there an A-board, discounts or adverts in local media. They supported a group of shops with late-night pre-Christmas promotion but by then the business was already profitable. It's just about having the right relationship with customers.

Blue Tit is only as good as the experience that each customer has with his or her stylist.

The company has a creative approach and operates different employment arrangements with each of its staff. One early member of staff is on a path to becoming a partner in the business and is now running the second salon. Some have bonuses, or take a proportion of the income they generate from customers. Another is expected to be a cost to the business but leads the professional development and training programme that has been developed for the team. All have flexible hours to enable them to pursue other interests.

A recent visit to the salon reminds me it is been almost two years since it first opened. Andi is due to go on holiday for five weeks: that will be his first proper break since opening the business. On his return, he says that he's expecting to have the money to open another salon. They are planning to expand and looking at a number of areas in London which are similar to Dalston. I wonder aloud whether they are going to raise money from investors. We are talking at cross-purposes. The new salon will be funded by the profits from this year's trading. No debt required. No equity sold.

If it's unlikely to be having a conversation with a hairdresser about the financials, it's even more unlikely to be discussing corporate expansion with someone like Andi. It's not just the scraggy beard that makes him seem unlike an entrepreneur. It's the relaxed attitude.

If he hadn't been raised near the Austrian mountains, his attitude would be more akin to a surfer's.

Blue Tit confounds many of the expectations around of what it takes to build a successful business. Their vision for the salon is clear. There isn't a clear business plan. Despite being a start-up, they are committed to contributing to their community. They have spent little on the salon and even less on marketing. Blue Tit focuses on giving customers the right experience with happy, relaxed staff. The business has taken care of itself. Andi and Perry have subjugated their own interests to the business, which has continued to grow as a result. And for as long as they can remain disciplined, and repeat their success of finding the right areas to open new salons, there will be Blue Tit salons in

other parts of the globe before long. Andi
fancies Rio.

Key points

- Andi and Perry spent as little as possible in setting up the salon – and launched before everything was in place.

- They were not dependent on the salon for their income.

- Their networks were sufficiently strong to guarantee them some customers.

- They knew enough about how and when people visit hairdressers to know that they would have some success at an early point.

Monitise – from 0 to £30m in three years

You read about people whose achievements are so considerable that they appear unreachable. There's little to learn because they're too good. But you don't get to meet them often. Or understand what actually makes them successful. Let me introduce you to Alistair Crane.

Alistair started a mobile apps business called Grapple. Its USP was that it would help you build an app which worked on several mobile phones (iPhones, Android and Blackberry all need apps written differently), dramatically reducing cost and time. But they wouldn't do this in competition with a large ecosystem of digital and mobile agencies. They would licence software to those agencies for them to build the apps.

I first met Alistair in March 2010. We were both in the first months of setting up our businesses. A mutual contact had introduced us to Fujitsu who invited us both to pitch to their sales team. One of their account directors introduced us to Whitbread.

I next saw Alistair two years later when I was settling down to watch The Apprentice on TV. The contestants were given a task to develop a mobile app – and were in the offices of Grapple to do it. So when I wanted to study a successful start-up, Alistair was the first person I would call. Our paths intersect once more. The day I publish the first edition of the book, Grapple is sold for a rumoured £35m. It's now part of mobile payments business, Monitise.

So what can you learn from Alistair? Some people say 'not much'. That he was lucky. A mobile apps business started in 2010 was always likely to succeed. So perhaps there isn't much to learn beyond: right place, right time. You evidently can't succeed if you are in the wrong place at the wrong time, so the reverse is a facile argument. The talent is getting in that situation. But once there, are you guaranteed success? Alistair's story is more complicated.

If there's a conventional method of starting a mobile apps business, it would launch from the safety of your bedroom. You would write a great app in your spare time. You could sell it to a company – or just give it to them in return for a great endorsement. Or you'd go straight to consumers through the app store. You'd carry on writing apps in your spare time until you had enough work to quit your day job and do it full time. You'd then grow the business by outsourcing the basic tasks to offshore developers.

That wasn't Alistair's secret. He didn't start the business on his own. Jamie True created the company. Jamie was a successful serial entrepreneur before the age of 35. He spotted the opportunity for making money out of mobile apps. Jamie came across a company in Canada called Cascada which was failing to make the most of its technology. He bought Cascada for about $1m and recruited Alistair to run the new company. That's quite the reverse of a bedroom start-up.

But just because it started with investment didn't mean that it lacked the spirit of a start-up. The company's early success wasn't the result of months' worth of meticulous planning. The company was registered in October 2009, Alistair appointed a director in January 2010 and it was trading by March.

There weren't endless iterations of mission statements. Business plans written and re-cut according to the needs of investors. There was no extensive competitor analysis or risk register. And there evidently wasn't time (or budget) wasted coming up with a good company name.

So Alistair didn't walk into the opportunity by converting a hobby into a business. But surely that meant that on day one he had to do the hard, time-consuming (and therefore expensive) work of generating sufficient interest and opportunities to land the first customer? Alistair did something smart to get going. Alistair started at Grapple when he was confident it would have a client. Time wasn't wasted operating in 'stealth mode'.

So Alistair had it easy because he had good financial backing and proven technology? Starting a business with financial backing does have benefits. But as Alistair puts it, if he hadn't been bringing in customers then by the third month the investors would have been tapping their watches. Investment buys software, not time. And the software was only proven in the sense that it worked. If it was *that* good, why hadn't the Canadian company been able to realise its potential?

Alistair soon found out. Grapple's customers didn't want the software Alistair was selling. Agencies didn't want to licence the software to build their own apps. They just wanted someone to do it for them. So Alistair stopped selling software licenses and started selling mobile apps.

I asked Alistair how long he spent hawking around a licence model to agencies. "About four weeks" he said. He didn't look for customers who wanted his products. He looked for products that his customers wanted. They'd just have to build the apps instead. It's a simple decision, the way that Alistair explains it. Yet one that many start-ups struggle to make. They shelter in the words of Thomas Edison – that he hadn't failed, just found 10,000 ways that something wouldn't work. So they persist.

The founder is emotionally invested in the idea. They've spent months talking about it. They've persuaded friends, investors and even themselves that their business plan is right.

When a customer says they don't want it, they say 'wrong customer' and move on to the next one. They keep looking for a market for their product.

There are some practical barriers towards changing direction. Lumbering start-ups have spent good money on a nice looking website. They've printed a brochure. They've got a strapline on their logo. They could change direction, and they might. But not now. There isn't the cash available to update the marketing straight away. The business has costs. The fuse is lit. The founder is running around trying to find a market.

Alistair lacked these inhibitions. It's not that he lacks emotional connection with the business. Despite showing due deference to Jamie as the founder it's very clearly Alistair's show. He describes himself as a "rockstar CEO". But if a client asked him to make ads rather than apps, he wouldn't blink. He's relaxed at highlighting the shortcomings of the company's early apps. He isn't passionate about the mobile apps market. He just wants to make money.

The first client was McCann Erickson. They were representing for Xbox. Alistair did everything possible to make sure they would become a client before leaving his job to start at Grapple. He didn't tell them that he was putting his career in their hands. But he got pretty close. And he showed similar diligence with its next clients. There was no time for a minimum viable product – just apps that people were prepared to buy. Alistair would personally visit their offices to make sure he got the contract signed. He'd wait there until it was. Lots of business founders would be too worried about looking like a one man band. Others worried about missing other opportunities. Alistair was focused on sales and immediate revenue.

Alistair has always been a salesman. He describes a childhood of weeding the driveway for extra pocket money whilst his friends were drinking cider in the local park. When I ask him what he would have done if the business had not worked, he's very clear: Got up and started again. He's supremely confident that he'd be able to sell a good product to anyone. That's an invaluable skillset lacking in too many entrepreneurs (British ones, at any rate).

But Alistair's career was a critical contributor to his start-up success. He may not be passionate about mobile apps in particular but he was a relative veteran of the mobile world. Alistair had previously been the first UK hire of a mobile start-up called Blyk. It offered free calls and text messages to customers willing to receive adverts instead. The company was then acquired by Nokia where Alistair became Head of Media Solutions.

The experience of working at a start-up was invaluable for Alistair. He was the first UK employee of Blyk. The only person left on the office floor when senior management huddled in the meeting room. It taught him about the culture of start-ups. How to build a dedicated team of experts who were willing to work long, hard hours for the enjoyment of building a business. That pizza and beer beats small salary increases for building staff loyalty.

It's a culture that still exists at Monitise: indeed, the business is based in the offices used by Blyk. I wonder aloud whether I've uncovered some secret motivation for Alistair in beating his former employers. But alas, it's because he knew that the space was free and he could get a good deal on the rent.

So Grapple wasn't just a good idea. Nor Alistair just an experienced salesman. He was right for the business. It was a logical step on his CV. Alistair's role at Nokia gave him a senior position at a company which had established relationships with the largest brands in mobile. When he moved to Grapple, he wasn't picking up the phone to strangers. They weren't a number in a directory. He didn't have to establish his personal credibility in the industry. His name wasn't a label for a cold-caller. Less tangibly, it placed Alistair at the heart of latest developments and opportunities in mobile marketing. He was well-placed to spot client demand for the next big thing. So he may be agnostic about mobile apps per se but mobile technology was a key part of his personal story, his relationships and his credibility.

Leaving behind the life of a salaried employee was not scary for Alistair. Entrepreneurship wasn't an alien concept. And Alistair does believe that personality, attitudes and skills have made him successful. Alistair believes that his drive and determination set him apart from equally capable, but less fearless peers who have stayed in more secure employment. He probably isn't talking metaphorically when he says he doesn't need an alarm clock to wake him up at 04.30. He can show you the work he did on Christmas Day. He usually works on Sundays too, but as a sign of Grapple's increasing maturity, he understands that he can't now expect to bother his team out of hours.

But now, after the sale, he draws a distinction with 'meathead entrepreneurs' who stress only how hard they work. He draws on relationships outside the world of the office and mobile technology. He tells of the time he spends reflecting alone. He points out the importance of working hard at the right thing, over working hard. And he tells tales of how his staff experiment with technology to try new things – ensuring a creative environment insulated from the daily pressure to deliver returns.

So Alistair understood that entrepreneurship wasn't just a state of mind but a way of behaving. Controlling costs was important. Alistair knew how to reach his customers. Personal contact would be essential; the first 12 clients and agency deals were all signed by Alistair himself.

Grapple didn't spend months developing thought leadership positions or sponsoring events or producing branded material. They had a basic website, a PowerPoint presentation and a book full of phone numbers. There's a nice interview of Alistair from September 2010 conducted via Skype with a small US tech blog. It's conducted from the Grapple offices. You know that because there's a logo behind Alistair's shoulder. It's printed on A4 paper on a standard colour LaserJet. Costs were firmly under control.

But he didn't confuse that with controlling growth. Whilst Alistair was wedded to the principles of spending only what was needed, he didn't confuse the principles with the means. Grapple decided to invest in public relations support within months. Before the summer, they had a full time PR expert employed as their seventh member of staff. The increased public profile meant that they didn't have to create all of the new business leads themselves. Businesses were serious about building apps, which meant a formal procurement process during which developers would be invited to tender. To get on the lists, Grapple had to be known. Strong case studies and PR to promote the company, and Alistair, was essential.

Grapple built a simple app for the Green Party. It wasn't Grapple's best piece of work that year, says Alistair. But it was a neat idea: a series of questions to identify how 'green' you were. And the party went on to win its first seat in parliament. A perfect case study for the business. And a great piece of PR: Grapple as part of a winning campaign.

It isn't fame, but money that motivates Alistair. He isn't archetypally British, middle class and embarrassed about it. His passion is fast cars and he wants to drive them and buy them. I don't know what he earned in his first few months of Grapple. But he didn't consider it a particular risk. He was sure that he could just go out, start again and find a different way of making money. It makes him dispassionate about the work that Grapple does. He wasn't embarrassed to say that its early apps were unsophisticated and I'm sure he wouldn't hesitate to tell a colleague when their work wasn't up to scratch.

Alistair isn't fussy. He greets me in person in reception, as he leaves another meeting. We are kicked out of an office by a junior colleague. The Grapple PR manager doesn't sit in on the meeting. In the early days of the business, he wasn't too clear about his status. It doesn't bother him. Jamie True is the founder of the company, as noted above. Alistair didn't fall in love with the name any more than he wanted to build apps. He can sound as coolly analytical as a management consultant on a temporary assignment. As a customer you'd have no doubt that he'd be on your side.

In summer 2010, less than a year after first trading, there were industry rumours of a bid for Grapple. The company was already thought to be worth over £10m. Grapple's PR campaign was in full swing. The company eventually sold for almost four times that number. So a linear path to a successful exit then? Not quite.

The 'pivot' from software licensor to app developer had a serious impact on the business model. The company ran out of cash that autumn. The company had invested in the staff necessary to build the business. Revenue growth was strong but costs were high. Fortunately, the investors were able to back the company. Alistair attributes some of this to the impact of the PR. That they were proud of their high profile investment and wanted to see it succeed.

The period reminded Alistair of the importance of profit over revenue. Having a 'strong user base', grateful and high profile clients and metres of media coverage feels nice. It doesn't pay the bills. The knowledge that people depended on him to pay their rent kept Alistair awake at night.

The story of the start-up that sold to Monitise isn't simple. It was hugely successful but contains lots of important lessons. It wasn't started in a teenager's bedroom. The CEO wasn't the founder but an industry expert with previous experience of start-ups. It was started with capital investment, but to buy technology that wasn't making enough money. The initial customer proposition failed. But the start-up worked for international brands within weeks. It was a valuable company within months. But its new business model almost killed the business.

So without proper analysis it's easy to assume that the company succeeded because it was in the right market at the right time. But it wasn't down to luck. And it wasn't all simple. But there are lessons which are valuable for any start-up in any sector, in any circumstance.

Alistair was the right person to run the business. He knew how to sell, he understood the market and he knew the right people. The large costs for an early-stage business, often the CEO's wages, weren't incurred before the business was confident of revenue. Alistair didn't hunt out a thousand rejections for the product. He found the right product for their market. And he invested in PR to buy the attention of his target market. He worried about the right things – customers, apps, hiring. He wasn't distracted by the naff name, the website design or whether the business was equipped to change direction. Alistair's passion was making money – making the business a success. And how he achieved.

Key points

- Alistair knew Grapple had a customer before quitting his job. He knew enough potential customers to be sure of reaching his target market.

- Alistair had experience of a start-up and strong professional credentials to run the business

- The business didn't take a product and look for a market. They found the market and looked for the right product

- They minimised the start-up costs and expected revenue in the first three months – but couldn't have survived without the PR campaign to reach their target market

- Starting a business with investment has its own challenges. It doesn't guarantee success or buy time

Bare Conductive: Finding the market for a new invention

Perhaps you think it's easy to see how James could grow a business out of home-made cooking. Maybe Andi and Perry were good hairdressers who got lucky in choosing Dalston for their first salon. Maybe Alistair's genius salesmanship, combined with good timing, was enough to remove the risk from the cost of acquiring their start-up technology.

So imagine that you begin your business in manufacturing. That the product you make has never been made before. That you start off with no money.

And your product isn't a 'must- have now' – at least not in the same way as food, haircuts or mobile apps.

That's what Becky Pilditch, Bibi Nelson, Matt Johnson and Izzy Lizardi did at Bare Conductive. They are not in the service industry. The product couldn't be constantly adapted to meet the needs of the market. There were some large costs of making the product. And if people didn't want it, there wasn't anything else they could make. But they were able to remove some of the key risks from starting their business. And they were quickly profitable.

These guys aren't just marginally successful. They are award-winning successful. The UK government's Technology Strategy Board recognised their success. The Shell Livewire competition has feted their achievements. And they've even been in a Calvin Harris video. Oh, and their product has sold in more than 50 countries.

It began at university. They were students on a course at the Royal College of Art that brought together designers and engineers, confronted them with real-world problems and encouraged them to adopt an entrepreneurial approach. In the post-graduate year, they had to complete a group project, demonstrated at an interim show, and then work on a more major solo project, profiled at graduation.

They didn't set out to start a business. They were interested in the human body. The course was about pushing frontiers. With technology so ubiquitous, what was next?

They were interested in how human skin could be used to conduct electricity. The team of four invented *paint* that conducted electricity.

The interim show generated some excitement for the idea on specialist technology blogs and amongst the 'maker' community – a US-led movement of enthusiastic amateur inventors and innovators. Then Becky spotted a conference in Eindhoven which seemed tailor-made to introduce their paint. She went along to present and the professor who organised it became a fan. His blog post generated considerable interest.

Back at university, at the end of year show Bibi got talking to Roger Ashby – a start-up guru who was at the event to look for interesting ideas with commercial potential Roger offered his help – and that of his colleague Rafat Malik.

The team were considering whether to take the idea forward when Sony Music got in touch. The company wanted to use the paint for the performance art in Calvin Harris' next video.

Bare Conductive became a registered company just in time to process the payment from Sony. It would have been a difficult decision – for some. They had just graduated and their debts were considerable. And most graduates are pretty keen to start work. But they all agreed. As Becky put it: 'What did we have to lose?'

Body paint for performing art was great at generating public attention but it was too small a market to launch a business. The revenues from Sony weren't significant but they were enough to start work.

They knew there were potential customers, and that others were capable of manufacturing their products. But the organic way the business came about meant that they didn't need to do formal market research. Becky knew that there wasn't anything else available on the market: competitors would have come to light following the Eindhoven conference. Large chemical companies such as Bayer would be only too capable of making the paint themselves, but the market was likely to be too small and too niche for it to attract their interest.

Developing conductive paint isn't like building mobile apps. The paint was good enough for the music video but it wasn't appropriate for a wider market.

The team spent the best part of the next year working on the formula and finding someone that would make it. They operated out of Matt's live-work studio and just managed to cover their expenses. The formula was perfected and they found a company that could make the paint. There were two main roles for the paint: body paint and product paint. They knew that paint for the body would have to undergo a different form of testing and licensing (it would be treated as a cosmetic), so they focused on the product paint. The manufacturers would require an order run of 20 litres, although the standard would be 100 litres. So there was little room for test and iteration once it was made. Becky explains that 'whether succeed or fail, we wanted to do so quickly'.

But the costs of starting the business were negligible. The prototype was delivered at university, using spare pockets of cash and the college equipment. The PR was done themselves. There was a very basic website. The brand was their own. No one was paid a salary. There was excitement and then demand for their product without a marketing budget or overheads. There wasn't a business card between them.

In October 2010, the Technology Strategy Board awarded Bare Conductive a prize of £100,000.

It arrived as the company was negotiating with investors to raise the capital needed to take the product to market. It meant that they could buy the machinery, without having to sell too much of their stake. Becky calls it luck – one of the key moments in the development of the business. It doesn't ring true. Winning a competitive, government competition can't be attributed to luck even if the timing was fortunate.

The business was all set to make its debut at the Maker Faire in New York, in Autumn 2010. The paint wasn't ready but they went to the event with a website launched and a stand to demonstrate proof of concept. Despite having no actual products to sell, they survived. The week the website launched, they received five orders. Bare Conductive was in business.

The team didn't identify the maker community through market research. They couldn't find them in the local pub. They couldn't reach them through Facebook ads. They were part of the community. The course at the Royal College of Arts – and their individual backgrounds in design and engineering – meant that they understood how to reach them. But the community isn't just a network of like minded individuals. It has a strong ethical core of early adopters with principles. Approach it in the wrong way and it would ruin the credibility of the business.

The mind-set of the maker community was part of the business. There had been an early discussion about making the recipe for the paint available as 'open source – publicly, freely available. They knew that there were more potential applications for their paint than they could possibly envisage. They wanted to discover how people would use it, interact with it – in short, they wanted to test what the paint could become.

A different mind-set would have produced a different business. The paint would have been a product component. They might have waited to discover its most valuable application. They might have specialised in a particular sector – cars, domestic lighting or circuit boards, for example. Instead, they had developed the minimum viable product. They had taken it to market as quickly as they could. And they had been as broad and generous as possible in their understanding of the market.

Pricing a new product isn't easy. The company knew how much it cost to manufacture, sort of. The cost of materials and production were factored in to the £18 price for a tin of the paint. The business wasn't paying the founders a full salary so pricing in the value of the research and development wasn't possible. But they wanted it to be affordable. And it was crucial that they sell it in small volumes, to allow people to experiment. They'll never know if it could have been £1 more expensive. But the price they did set made them a profit.

Within six months, the business had launched its next products. They'd attracted interest from schools and educators who wanted to use the paint to teach people physics in a different way. They developed kits for schools which proved very popular and brought the concept to a new generation of makers.

The principles of good design remain core to the business. The next big product launch was a pen that gave customers greater control over the paint and meant that it could be applied in finer detail. It built on the greetings cards which were also proving to be popular.

The largest order arrived in early 2013 – for 14,000 pens. The company decided to fulfil the order in-house, as they tended to do. Whilst assembling 14,000 ink pens may have many people waking up in a cold sweat, the founders of Bare Conductive saw it as a significant opportunity to learn about the assembly and distribution process. They had previously learnt a lot about how to box a product by doing it themselves, and the experience of making the pens encouraged them to reduce the number of constituent parts.

People familiar with stories of Apple Inc (the computers, not the Beatles) may recognise some similarity with that company's obsession with elegant design. The detailed understanding of the process and the need for simplicity and focus on the user certainly sounded closely related. That's what great designers do.

With so many potential applications, remaining focused was a challenge. It's one they still wrestle with. But with professional training in engineering and design, they are also well-equipped to understand how to tackle it. The founders don't have to set aside particular time for research and development in the way that Google do. It's just what they do.

The business model that supports product development reflects their iterative ways of working. They have hundreds of conversations with people intrigued by what they do. Where they spot opportunities they develop products to be able to show customers how they would work. And then they secure orders to develop their new ideas. The founders are sufficiently well-networked that they understand what excites potential customers whilst being expert enough to anticipate what they have to do in order to give them what they need.

The role of the founding chairman, Roger Ashby, and his colleague Rafat 'cannot be over-stated', according to Becky. It's not just politeness. Were it not for Roger's suggestion, the chances are they would not have created Bare Conductive. And with previous experience of start-ups, he is able to help the team with fundraising and legal issues as well as the commercial elements of running the business.

The team can also draw on the experiences of their friends and network from the Royal College of Art. Becky says she knows other businesses that had to raise money to get going and have struggled to match the rapid growth of Bare Conductive. She is glowing about the support and behaviour of the external investors they found, suggesting the shared vision for the business has helped them grow.

Despite hitting some significant milestones, Becky says they don't really have time to reflect. Bibi says it's because "there's always the next thing to do". They are in a hurry. They founded the business with an intention of building something to sell. Now they've established revenue, they are in a position to earn a decent salary from the business.

So who are these ruthless business people who've developed a product from scratch and sold it globally? Four student friends.

Bikes hang from the ceiling of the office. They share a group of desks. They know each other as well as university flatmates. They've different professional skills – and appear to have very different personalities. They've been brilliant at PR without learning the skills or hiring the expertise. They've become proficient at sales without a commercial background. The finances are watched carefully and potential staff have been hired with considerable care. And they've learnt that all en route.

Bare Conductive were passionate about a product. It brought them together and gave them the public profile which created the company. They made sure the product worked and then went all out to make sure it sold. The finances did not resemble a three year plan but operated on a hand-to-mouth basis until they had created enough value to raise investment. When the product launch came, it wasn't quite ready. But the business worked anyway.

The company reduced the risks inherent in a start-up as far as it could. Its approach was very similar to the others in this book, despite a very different business model. The founders were experts: they had created something no one else had made. It was all they had to sell and they were fascinated to spot the best opportunity for it.

But their paint could do anything. Start-ups usually need focus, a single solution to a particular problem, a clearly defined 'offer' to customers which they can understand. The more complex the pitch, the harder the sale. Yet Bare Conductive had a blank canvas.

They avoided the pitfalls of specialisation. The team could have waited months, trying to find the killer application for the paint. But how many months? And what if they hadn't?

Getting paint to customers was the priority. They would figure it out: their understanding of the maker community – their customer base – meant that they knew they could show them the way and let them create. Incidentally, the business still grapples with the need to focus against the massive potential for the paint. There's no simple answer but the fact that they constantly examine it is probably enough.

The financial cost was limited. The founders did not take cash out of the business until it was generating its own revenue. The first order, from Sony, came at the start of the business' life and provided enough cash to develop the product. By the time they made the first batch of paint, they didn't have the certainty of orders that was available to Grapple. But they knew that they'd done enough to generate demand.

They were as confident as Blue Tit was that they were able to get some early customers. And as Bim's Kitchen knew they could sell jars at farmers' markets, Bare Conductive knew they could sell tins of paint at the Maker Faire.

Bare has some core costs which were a necessary part of bringing its product to market – just like Grapple and Blue Tit. It couldn't avoid the cost of manufacturing as Bim's Kitchen did. And it couldn't manufacture a small, test amount to test the consumer market. If its paint could not be commercialised, they did have the intellectual property which had given Grapple so much confidence.

Bare took off because it could make the paint cheaply enough; it had already recognised the appeal it had amongst the maker community. Success was not inevitable, however, and the risk was high. A different set of decisions would have prevented them from bringing the product to market. If they had launched the paint before it was ready in order to capitalise on the PR from the Calvin Harris video, they may have failed. If they had each taken a salary whilst developing the paint, it would have failed. If they'd spent a long time trying to find the killer application that proved the potential of the paint, it might have taken too long, and not have impressed the market.

Selling the paint was a natural part of their story. But it was a brilliant part of the business. And if they'd spent their capital on developing a suite of products, fewer of them might have worked. They've currently released only those products for which there is demand.

And they've done this all without any nonsense, without any airs and graces or great pretensions. They have complementary roles. No one is jostling for position. They are all founders. They all get on. Each recognises the other's expertise. And they remain a cohesive group. It, they, couldn't be further from 'The Apprentice'. They've not just made a real business but created a market out of magical black paint.

Key points

- Bare Conductive knew there was interest in their product before they decided to start the business.

- The business had a sale from Sony which covered the initial expense of developing the product.

- They managed to live on minimal funds until the product was ready.

- They had a tightly defined, clear niche about which they were passionate but a generous and broad view about what people could do with the product.

- Once launched, they wasted no time in marketing and selling the product,

- They were experts at every stage of the product development, manufacturing and even distribution.

- They only made new products for which there was a clear market demand.

13 rules for success

It's like the start of a bad joke: what do the hairdresser, the designer, the chef and the mobile guru have in common? Only it doesn't end in the way I expected. They didn't all have a secret start-up failure in their past. They didn't all have pots of cash from an inheritance. They didn't all have a great idea for a killer product that would revolutionise the market.

The contrast between me and these founders was not immediately obvious, apart from the blindingly obvious factor that they had a product for which there was a demand. They weren't successful because they were expert sales people and I wasn't. They weren't all more driven, committed or hard-working than me. They didn't just choose to take fewer risks, breaking into an established market rather than trying to do 'something new'.

There was a chance that they simply got lucky. Grapple launched at the right time in the mobile apps business, before later being purchased by Monitise. Blue Tit found the right point in the Dalston property boom.

Bare Conductive happened to meet Roger. But those were parts of their story.

They weren't the difference between success and failure. Whether we'd launched Newscounter two years earlier or later, it still wouldn't have been successful. We weren't one meeting away from building a customer base. So no, luck wasn't the distinguishing factor in the successful stories compared with Newscounter's tale of woe.

What's a mistake? It should be an easy question to answer. I could go for the all-embracing answer: everything I did. Newscounter was a mistake. It generated no revenue and therefore everything we did was a mistake. That isn't a particularly satisfactory answer, however: many of the day to day things we did at Newscounter we repeated at Trufflenet with a different outcome. Even if everything important at Newscounter was a mistake, some of it led to the relationships which brought about Trufflenet. So it can't have all been bad.

Instead, I could answer give the minimal, but factually correct answer: the idea. The idea was wrong so everything that flowed from that was never going to be right. That makes more intuitive sense. We were powerless to make right a broken idea. It still feels inadequate as a response because of the number of people who shared our confidence in the idea. It also doesn't excuse why we didn't spot the failings of the idea, or why we couldn't have created a successful business out of a different idea.

Not all mistakes were disastrous. Some enabled us to get better. If we hadn't have got the first website design wrong, we wouldn't have known how to get the second right. And without a design, we wouldn't have had something to critique. So whilst Newscounter may not have been a credible business it allowed me to talk to corporate communicators about reputational challenges. That led to the PR agency asking for social media monitoring. So it wasn't all a mistake and it wasn't fundamentally a mistake.

It was easy to identify the serious mistakes: they cost time and money. Money runs out, time can't be replaced. Spending money on the wrong thing is annoying and regrettable but is often unavoidable. It is (usually) done out of a misunderstanding of the market or a poor analysis of the problem, not a basic failure of approach.

I truly understood what my most serious errors were only when I studied the success of first-time entrepreneurs. I made avoidable mistakes because they were based on a lack of knowledge. I could have known and I didn't. To paraphrase Donald Rumsfeld, I didn't know that I didn't know. I was blind.

The successful entrepreneurs had 13 things in common. And each confronted expectations about successful start-ups.

#1 You have to be right for the business

'Find the Business in You' implores the government advertising campaign. Anyone can start a business. There's no single type of entrepreneur. There are young ones, old ones. Entrepreneurs who were good at school. Entrepreneurs who left school as soon as they could. There are powerful, forceful entrepreneurs and modest and self-effacing ones (honestly!).

The truisms continue. The only thing standing in the way of you and your dream is you. People who are successful are those prepared to take a risk. If you make the jump, you may surprise yourself with how much you can achieve. You can prove it to yourself and change the destiny of your life, and your family's fortunes.

The idea that a billboard on Old Street and some formulaic advice can help people start a business is eccentric. Some might even consider it a poor use of government funds. It takes more than that to change behaviour. But what's worse is the idea that *anyone* can start a business. It is offensive to those who succeed.

Others argue that entrepreneurs are, well, entrepreneurial. That it doesn't matter who you are but what you are. Whether you are the sort of personality to start a business. Entrepreneurs aren't the sort of people to sit and wait for a good idea. They just get out there and do it. Help is available for those who seek it. There is advice on writing a business plan, on protecting intellectual property and raising money. Give the right personality the right environment and they will make a successful business.

But starting a business also requires particular skills. You can't discover if you've got the skills without using them. But you can't expect to have the skill because you do it. Otherwise park footballers would be playing in stadiums. There are some skills that are universally useful to a start-up. If you can do basic bookkeeping, you'll save the cost of getting someone else to do it. If you know the basics of employment law, you won't have to pay for advice. If you run a shop and are a dab-hand at decorating or fixing the electrics, you'll save some cash on the side.

Writing this book taught me that making a success of a business requires knowledge. That can be taught and learnt. But simply setting up a business with neither the skills nor the knowledge is foolhardy.

It's also phenomenally risky. You can lose everything. That doesn't mean you will, of course, but it's sensible to limit your liability. But even then people risk chasing their losses. The harder the business becomes, the more tempting it is to re-mortgage the house. Your pension will suffer regardless. And even if you don't lose any cash, there's a decent chance you've damaged your career and lost potential earnings. Your CV will deter some employers, assuming you are a lone maverick. Others will assume you are just looking to steal their ideas. Even if you can get a job, others will have been promoted ahead of you. Too few businesses value and know where to direct the start-up skill set.

There are times in your life when it's better to start a business. If you need spare capital, you aren't likely to have that in the early years of owning a house. To devote yourself to a start-up whilst you have young children is controversial. To raise significant investment as a young person without a track record is highly unlikely.

I tried all three. Wedded to a failing business simply to pay a mortgage. Married, with a baby soon after, so dependent on a salary. And too young and inexperienced to give confidence to investors that I was capable of running a company with the larger sums we needed to raise at Trufflenet.

So the odds are bleak. There probably *isn't* a business in you. The government may not be best-placed to know whether you are ready to start a business. You may not have the skills or knowledge. It may be the wrong time of life. And you may not have the right idea for a business. And if you have all of them, there's no guarantee of success. And if you aren't successful, no one will give you special treatment for trying. Just the same jobseekers allowance available to every other desperate sod.

But there's something more fundamental. You need the specialism to start a business. You have to be good at something core to the business. You have to be part of the value of the business. The successful entrepreneurs were experts in their field.

There are two immovable requirements at the heart of a start-up: first, you have to make a product that people want; second, you have to sell it. Some great innovators can't sell, so never have a business. Some great sales people never have the product idea to start their own business. You don't need to specialise in both in equal measure. Just enough of one, and lots of the other, to prove there's a viable business. There are no founders who do not have a specialism. The person who can neither make the product nor sell it is the pub bore – constantly droning on about the brilliant idea he's had and he can't believe why no one has done it already.

I was no better than the pub bore. Newscounter was a website but I had no experience in building one so we had to hire someone to help. It needed someone to sell to corporate communicators. And I couldn't do that. And we couldn't afford to buy that specialism. When I hired someone to make the initial phone calls, it hadn't even occurred to me I was passing off the most important part of the job: speaking to customers. I thought being willing to work hard was valuable. I thought that being able to apply myself to a range of tasks was rare. And I thought I could make do on the rest. We had to pay for the product to be made *and* I wasn't able to sell it. It was a toxic combination.

I wasn't any better suited to Trufflenet initially. It was a technology provider – and I couldn't do that. The software service needed to be sold – and I couldn't do that. Only when it became a consultancy service, supported by compelling research, could I contribute something valuable. But by then it was too late. Expensive bills had been paid.

So you've got everything in place to start a business. You are a specialist in your field. You can make the thing your business will sell. Your rent is low and you don't have any dependents. You are prepared to leave abstemiously for the next year. Is that enough to start a business?

Not anyone can start a business nor can someone start any business. There are ideas that are beyond the reach of most entrepreneurs. Richard Branson started an airline, but only after having cash to invest and a track record of success which gave investors' confidence that he could make a good stab at doing so. I may want nothing more than to manufacture hover-boards to revolutionise local transport. I may have the technical expertise to manufacture a prototype (alas, I don't). But I don't have the track record to warrant investment, and neither do I have enough cash myself to do it. Hopefully a reader does. (You know where I am.)

If it all sounds terribly unfair, it is. Entrepreneurship isn't a golden ticket. A killer idea from an average Joe can't create the next Facebook. You need to be right, the circumstances need to be right and the business needs to be right. But do that right, and you are on the next rung of the ladder. Get it very right and you can be investing in hover-boards.

Believing anyone can start a business was my first mistake. I was too expensive; unable to make the product we had to sell, increasing the cost of going into business.

I was a drain on resources, unable to afford to live on nothing whilst the business grew. The wrong person, doing the wrong thing at the wrong cost.

Successful entrepreneurs have a talent. The team at Bare Conductive were brilliant designers, and found support and backing from a leading institution in their field. The conductive paint was a breakthrough technology. But you don't have to be a brilliant product inventor. Alistair Crane could sell anything, for example. He understood the mobile world better than most. He had connections with many of the people that he needed to buy his company's services. James Adedeji made delicious cooking sauces. He had picked up enough tips on how to do PR that he was pretty good at that. And he was very good at listening to his customers. Andi and Perry had a clear vision, a talent for cutting hair and a strong network of customers and potential employees. They, like Alistair, also had the benefit of having worked in a start-up environment previously.

Successful entrepreneurs do not have to be equally adept at developing a product, marketing and sales. But without a core skill at one of those things they merely have an idea. A pipe dream. The cost of buying those skills in other people is very high. It puts the business at risk. It makes the start-up less likely to work.

#2 Entrepreneurship isn't a full time job

You can't run a business by halves. You have to be passionate. You have to be focused. It's a risk but you get nothing without trying. It's a bigger risk not to try. You can't do that in your spare time. You work 40 hours a week. You need a bit of a weekend. Once you've done the household chores there's not much spare time. You have to sleep.

Lots of jobs don't allow you to do another. Employers worry that you won't concentrate, that you'll be stealing business from them that you'll get too ambitious. They won't be able to handle the request. HR doesn't have a form for someone wanting to start their own business.

You might like to moonlight. But your start-up needs the exposure. You need to get your name out there. You need to start making waves – getting in the news, getting on the phone. Even if HR doesn't notice, your boss is bound to.

Then there's the mortgage. And the bills. And your family. You need to look smart. You need to keep the lights on. There's phone and Internet access – you can't be without those. And you can't pick the right time of life to start a business. You wish you were a student, but you aren't. When you are 50, you might not have the energy.

These aren't simple issues. Few businesses can be run at the weekends. HR departments aren't renowned for their flexibility. Neither are mortgage companies. Running a business is neither discrete nor discreet. You don't want to raise the issue and find yourself sacked before the start-up is ready. You don't want to be sacked for gross misconduct either.

Creating a business isn't the same as getting a job. Starting a business is a compromise. You can't eliminate risk for the business or you. You can't achieve perfection. You have to forget what could have been. But when you are deciding how you are going to setup a business and pay the bills there's one compelling constraint: money. You can only do that which you can afford to do. If you haven't the money to pay yourself, you haven't the money. You can't risk being sacked pre-emptively. You can't risk paying your whole salary if the business hasn't the cash.

It is a dilemma. But understand it clearly. I
didn't. I thought I had to be paid. Even the
£1,000 a month I took felt like a sacrifice. I
thought I had to be full-time. And I thought it
would take time to make a success of the
business. And I didn't understand the tension
between these three things.

I was in a salary strangle. I wasn't being paid
enough to keep living but I was taking enough
from the business to kill it. Don't become a
leach. Stop taking the money. Or better still,
don't start: take only when you are adding.
And do it when the business can afford it, not
when your pocket requires it. So there's a
choice. Either don't start a business, or start
the business you can afford to start.

Bim's Kitchen worked around this principle.
By developing his sauce business whilst
working full time in the Department of
Health, James ensured that he could find out
whether the idea, whether his talents, could
sustain a business. Alistair Crane didn't quit
his job at Nokia until he knew that Grapple
had its first customer. Most starkly, Andi and
Perry at Blue Tit were ready to live in relative
poverty to build the business.

You can earn a lot of money. In a comfortable job. Or you can get your dream job. Just as long as you don't want to earn much. Founding a business just may not be for you.

#3 Companies with bad names make more money

Entrepreneurs can spend hours, days, weeks and months deliberating over a business name. Or spend thousands of pounds. Or both. It feels like such a critically important decision.

It must be memorable. It's helpful if it intrigues the listener – or tells them what you do. Better still, if it becomes a catch-all term for your industry: think Hoover or Google.

Maybe it's got to work if someone hears it by word of mouth. Perhaps it's got to be pronounceable on the radio. You'll want people to spell it correctly. It's irritating enough when your own name is spelt wrongly.

Perhaps your name goes into the logo. Or does that make it sound a bit small-scale? Maybe you want something bland enough to allow expansion. Or is expansion only going to come if you've got a name that's so compelling that people want to talk about your business.

Then there's the domain. You really want to buy the dot com. You want to make sure customers will be able to email you easily. You certainly don't want to find that they might end up on a competitor's website. Or that you'll never be listed in the top 10 search results. Perhaps you want a short Twitter handle or a good Facebook page name. Certainly you want to make sure that someone else hasn't got it.

What about the logo? Something striking. Something simple. Something that speaks to the values of your brand.

It's got to be the right colour. Perhaps the logo needs to be visible as a little icon on Twitter. Or maybe it's important that it doesn't offend people in other countries.

I had two great names. Neither were my idea. But both worked fabulously well. Newscounter worked aurally. Black and white speech bubbles provided a powerful logo which encapsulated our brand values. Trufflenet was even better: rooting out value. Highly trained experts sorting out the value from the dirt. We could bring truffles (not those ones) to new business meetings. That helped people remember and it made us friends amongst PAs – critical to getting those phone calls answered later on.

Newscounter took months, and eventually a couple of thousand pounds in branding costs. We had wanted to be called 'the right to reply' but couldn't afford to buy the dot.com domain name. Trufflenet took longer still – rebranding wasn't complete until three months after launch, in fact. The name emerged one day from a breakfast with a friend who we then commissioned to produce the logo for a small sum. Until we had Trufflenet, we knew that the name wasn't perfect. But it hadn't stopped us spending lots of money on marketing materials which we then had to throw away.

Grapple Mobile is a rubbish name. It says nothing about apps. Bim's Kitchen could be mistaken as a kitchen waste receptacle. Blue Tit has a logo that could be mistaken for

Twitter's. And what's that to do with hairdressing anyway. Bare Conductive suggests nakedness, possibly through dance. Conductive suggests heat to me – not electricity.

They made money, though. We didn't.

It is not about the names. A great name that no one has heard of is not a great business. A great name for a terrible product makes a terrible business. A great name that costs thousands won't generate a return for a start-up.

It is about the mind-set. These businesses didn't spend time and money investing in a great name. They spent time and money investing in a great brand. Founders who spend ages deliberating a name is wasting time that could be better spent on marketing. They need to be talking to people, trying out the name and seeing what reaction they get. Just choose something and get on with it. Find out if it will do. You can always rebrand but you can never recover lost time.

Businesses with bad names make more money because they spend time talking to customers and investing in what the name means.

Those that don't are just hiding, talking to themselves, putting off the day of discovery.

#4 92% of time on your business plan is wasted

'The best businesses are less likely to have started with a business plan than they are by founders who jumped into the fray and just started doing.'

Hearts, Smarts, Guts and Luck: What It Takes to Be an Entrepreneur and Build a Great Business (Anthony K. Tian et al, Harvard Business Review Press, 2012)

Starting a business encourages planning. A plan anticipates a course of events. For X to happen, I need to do Y. But what if step one is broken? What if it doesn't lead the business towards step two? A traditional plan provides contingencies, even damage limitation, but only within the original frame. What if the expectations were wildly wrong?

Plans have an end. The more distant the end, the greater the guesses in the plan. For a start-up, even a year is longer than sensible. But a plan for a short period is just a timetable, a sequence of activities. With so much dependent on other people, you can miss the target without it being your fault.

Whatever you do, don't write a business plan. There is nothing good about them. They defer decisions and reinforce pointless knowledge. They hide what you don't know. They do not serve as a plan for your business. They are as relevant to your small start-up as the standing orders of the local neighbourhood watch committee.

Business plans are often written to templates. You'd never dream of using Microsoft Office templates, so why would you bother using a template for something that seems so crucial? They're just generic bureaucracy, written to a formula that is so old, no one can trace its origins. In fact, the original authors are probably too ashamed to admit to their success on Wikipedia. Anonymously.

If business plans had any financial value, there would be academic research on them conducted by serious psychologists. These studies would demonstrate the damage to your brain caused by writing them. Most start-up businesses write a business plan. Most start-up businesses fail.

Business plans are useful for bank managers, people who don't run a business and don't know how to. People with less responsibility and relevant experience than the owner of your local shop (or the manager of said Tesco Metro). That means they aren't useful for you.

Business plans begin with an explanation of your product. It's a logical starting point and it feels good to be able to articulate on paper what your product is and why people want it. By that point you'll have thought about it so much that the task will be easy and feel like progress.

But you don't have a clue about your product. It's an unlabelled seed without compost. Until your product has had its first encounter with the market, you don't know what it will look like. After your first few outings, you may be pretty keen to change your product as fast as you can.

Business plans aren't even useful for heaven's sake. They usually contain a section on marketing. But until you start up, you don't *know* whether adverts will be more effective than phone calls; emails better than letters; industry conferences better than press coverage. Adopting one route over any other is as effective as playing 'pin the tail on the donkey'. You can't execute a plan based on your ill-informed marketing decisions because you have no idea how long it will take to prove that route A is more effective than route B.

But the biggest sin of all is that business plans are an exercise in deceit. There's no space on the form to say 'this is what I don't know'. But such a section would have been the only useful starting point.

That requires a massive leap for most founders. You haven't set up a business because you are racked in self-doubt. You haven't told your partner that you've gambled your income prospects on a vague punt. And that's why it such a powerful point of departure.

There *is* good news, though. Most people don't want to read your business plan. I've never met an investor who's said 'show me your business plan' (though I've never raised finance from a bank). I've never met a non-executive director who's said 'show me your business plan'. I've never met a client who's said 'show me your business plan'.

There are lots of moments when you may think you've started a business. When you register at Companies House. When your business cards arrive. When you tell people you've started a business. When you quit your job. You haven't.

Our plan ceased to have value on day two. We hadn't planned for silence. We expected someone to be interested. But they weren't. We had no contact with customers and barely any website hits. There was no obvious interest in the business, no hope of hitting revenue targets for the month. But nothing to suggest growth wasn't possible. How to bring it about? We needed a plan – just not the one we had.

All we had were complex relationships. We aren't going to get customers until we've got enough website visitors. We can't get those until the website is interesting. We can't get that until we've got customers.

Progress could come from anywhere. But at Newscounter, there was nothing to build on. We could do anything or nothing. Should we do more of something or less of something else? Were we too broad or too specific? What if we spent months chasing the wrong opportunity? We didn't know whether the target was at fault or our aim. Or whether both were right and it just needed more familiarity. If potential customers were opening their emails then over time they'd anticipate their arrival. And surely then it would lead to interest. But how long would that take? Guessing was futile.

We needed small, independent goals. A conversation with a customer. Someone interested in the website. A journalist writing about the content. An email reply asking for more information. Not so much a plan, as a series of small achievements. Could we get a blogger interested in the right to reply? Would another website be interested in one of our stories? How many hits would persuade a communications department to answer our emails? All valid questions, but many steps from revenue.

With income so distant, what represented progress? It's hard to measure whether a brand is high profile and harder still to know whether it's enough. Reputations can be established in moments. But no one could say what would be enough to generate income, or how long it would take.

Perhaps we didn't know enough. Only by starting could we discover whether there was interest. Only by starting could we discover long it would take to build momentum. And now we had we knew we were starting from the ground up.

The costs arrived each month. There was evidence of progress if you looked hard enough. But without income there was nothing to determine whether it was enough. Would bits of contact build relationships that produced money?

The alternative is to not have any expectations. To learn the art of the possible. Expect nothing and surprise yourself. Aim higher and repeat. It's modest and unassuming. And they happen to be two key attributes of successful businesspeople. (But don't let that sway your decision-making.)

There is a moment of truth. When your business begins, and you start trading. Not when you pay the first bill.

When the first sale is secured. I know, by that harsh measure, Newscounter never made it. But this is why it's so important. The sooner you get there, at the lowest possible cost, the higher your chances of success.

Bare Conductive, Bim's Kitchen, Blue Tit and Grapple stand out because they got there quickly. They had a business before they had a plan. Form followed function. We can't all be that fortunate – that talented. But we can learn from their approach.

Grapple started with probably the most sophisticated plan and its entire business model was turned upside down within the first four weeks of trading in 2009. Blue Tit never had a plan, and they continue to make significant returns. Bare Conductive spent six months after their first customer perfecting their product – and they couldn't predict how long it would take. A traditional business plan is pointless.

#5 Love-struck entrepreneurs lose money

'Big ideas are very exciting and they seem to possess some kind of magic power that blinds people to common sense.'

43 Mistakes Businesses Make – And How to Avoid Them (Duncan Bannatyne, Hodder Business Plus, 2011)

Many businesses begin when the entrepreneur falls in love. It's a brilliant idea. It came and went in a thunderbolt moment. You have lots of ideas, of course, but unlike the others, this one kept coming back. You couldn't shake it. You'd mention it after dinner. It would wake you up in the middle of the night. It just wouldn't go away. The more you thought about it, the more compelling it became.

You are passionate about your idea, about your business. You want the whole world to share in your passion. You are an evangelist. You want people to benefit from your marvellous insight. If only more people saw the world your way, it would be a better place. You do not try to see the world through their cynical eyes but to open theirs to your world. Eventually, your nearest and dearest get frustrated. They tell you to put up or shut up. So you do. It generates an unstoppable momentum. Your idea becomes a business.

And that love will make you do all sorts of things. It was the safety net you needed to take the plunge. It makes you work hard. It enables you to talk with passion about your idea to investors, customers.

To persuade suppliers and staff to go the extra mile. Your love pushes you forward to do things of which dreams are made.

If I hadn't fallen in love, I wouldn't have set up Newscounter. Everywhere we looked we saw applications for our service. Love blinded us to the nuance. We didn't see the hesitation on people's faces. We just heard affirmation. We had lost our curiosity. There was an opportunity to confirm our prejudices around every corner. Reading news headlines made me deeply frustrated that we weren't there to help (or rather take advantage of) the situation. We didn't examine objectively how our potential customers managed without us. There was a gap in the market. But we didn't ask why. We didn't talk to the potential customers. We assumed we knew what they would say. We just needed to get on and do it.

Falling in love excuses many failings. At Newscounter, we didn't want the idea to be wrong; we *willed* it to be right. Minor quibbles faded into the distance. Even major problems became assimilated into the love story. Aren't the struggles what makes you great? If you are in love, you will genuinely believe it. But business isn't sentimental. It's not even about honesty. It is about objectivity.

Writers are advised to cut out their favourite phrases. Entrepreneurs should cut out their most cherished ideas.

We were a little wrong about a lot. When these little mistakes were assembled, the idea had the substance of a paper house. There were some stories that misrepresented organisations. Just not 10 a day. Some were serious enough to warrant action, but not three a day. A few of these were a problem because the organisation lacked the right of reply, but not one that they'd pay to correct. Cumulatively, these didn't make enough to form the basis of a lively news website, let alone a regular income. Once or twice a month there were organisations that were sufficiently upset about the story to do something about it. These cases were so serious that our service was inadequate. But we also valued the wrong things. Even-handedness was not considered important by any of our audiences. Awareness of the website could not have been built through regular media coverage. Journalists thought that their readers weren't interested in reading about the news.

I was sentimentally attached to the project. Each detail was important. I was convinced about our approach but had lost the purpose amongst the detail. If we had found value from some part of what we did, I wouldn't have spotted it. I was infatuated.

If you market your product to enough people, for long enough, someone will pay eventually. Email spammers build fraudulent businesses on that basis. But that isn't sustainable. That's a one-night stand. I learnt later that 10 'nos' is enough. The sign need to change. Success doesn't come to those who wait, but those who adapt.

Love is a barrier to change. You are so infatuated, you fail to notice the warning signs. You see green shoots and get your hopes up. You see the customer's friendly greeting, not their lukewarm commitment to 'stay in touch'.

Love makes a poor sales pitch. I met people to sell my idea. It's a simple conversation. You have an idea to sell. They don't like it. Err, that's it. There's nowhere to go. Nothing more to say. When they don't want it, you can only move on to the next one.

We could change everything except the idea. Change the patter and the customers would drop into place. Re-write the email and the replies would arrive. Free trials gave an impression of validity. It was a door-opener but it didn't deliver sales, so we improved the follow-up. These were solutions of the desperate. We didn't fail to listen, but we did fail to understand.

There is heroism in being right in the face of all adversity. It's one of the oldest stories known to mankind. And it reads as well in business. There are just enough stories to make it plausible that a business can break through despite apparently insurmountable barriers. That's what the social sciences call a 'survivor bias.'

Business clichés mislead. Anita Roddick *did* build a successful business after being refused start-up capital because the bank deemed the risk too high. James Dyson faced bankruptcy, lawsuits and thousands of product designs before eventually making a success of his vacuum cleaner. In those stories, your heart yearns for the obvious lesson: that their passion conquered a battalion of cynics. Your brain needs to learn the hard lessons. That the proposition Anita Roddick showed her bank manager may not have been worthy of funding. That Dyson's original vacuum cleaners may not have been the brilliant, sexy tools that they eventually became. Both adapted again and again finding new ways of surmounting their challenges. And other businesses came and went, changing the environment – the market – for The Body Shop and Dyson.

Love is a barrier to self-criticism. You will have a strange emotional attachment to all sorts of things that just make for bad business. It may be the logo that no one likes or the name that no one can pronounce. It is hard enough not to throw good money after bad without having an irrational attachment to processes that you follow and propositions from your business.

The business of love may be lucrative. Loving your business isn't. It's a barrier to change. An instinct to stop you following the money. It's hard to be in love with an idea and to jettison it for a more opportune one. If you've just spent months telling people that your idea is the best way to fix a problem, you probably believe it. You may believe in your idea so strongly, you don't want to quit. You may even want to continue doing the business with minimal signs of success because you feel so passionately about the idea. That's fine. It's called charity. But even charities need to persuade other people to part with their cash.

When we abandoned Newscounter to pursue the social media monitoring concept that would become Trufflenet, I was concerned. I wondered what I was doing. We would be offering social media monitoring. That wasn't what I wanted to do. I had fallen in love with a totally different idea and had no comparable love for the new concept. This was just a business. It wasn't going to change the world.

Sure, I wanted to see it work. My debt to our loyal investors was motivation enough.

I also wanted to prove that I had the ability to land a few sales. I was scared of being unemployed. But at best I was agnostic about the idea. It didn't keep me awake at night. I would work long hours – but not on a personal crusade to change the world.

My lack of love saved the business. When something didn't work, we changed it. I was more impartial advisor than evangelist. Objectivity made me much better at making informed decisions about Trufflenet. I could recommend actions to the board and analyse the state of the business without confusing the job of protecting shareholder interests (which included my own) with my passion for an idea. When I made mistakes, it was because I couldn't see an alternative, not because I didn't want to.

We asked our customers what they wanted. We listened to their response. The first said we needed a different layout. They got it. The second wanted email alerts. They got it. The third wasn't interested in the web-based interface, they wanted a report. Seeing that report gave more confidence to the fourth client, who wanted a project rather than an ongoing feed. By the sixth client, we weren't even selling a web interface. We just sold research projects. We weren't precious about doing it our way, we did it their way.

We gave them what they wanted. And we offered it to more people.

It did take time to find a passion, and a way of channelling that. I am now fascinated by the sector, the challenge of handling big data and the way we communicate that to clients. I get excited about the possibilities of providing ground-breaking new services to clients. I get excited by winning new business and investigating new areas of public attitudes. I like the Trufflenet name. I'm frustrated that we don't have a higher profile when people that do have one use it to such poor effect.

But I'm not in love with the business.
Deciding to leave was not tricky.

So being in love was a disaster. It left us reaching for a perfection that didn't exist. It meant that we continued to develop a product that no one wanted, and it blinded us to the failings. We desperately needed to change and we couldn't because we had gone into business to pursue the wrong thing.

Alistair Crane didn't like mobile apps. He was interested in the business, not the product. James Adedeji clearly loved cooking. But he was sufficiently dispassionate that he was able to abandon his best-seller in favour of building a more distinctive, African-inspired brand.

#6 Making money doesn't wait
'Few undertakings actually meet their founders' bullish expectations. Life has a tendency to interrupt. So many of us believe we are better at predicting the future than we really are.'

Start It Up: Why Running Your Own Business is Easier Than You Think (Luke Johnson, Penguin Portfolio, 2011)

It's a start-up cliché that it takes time to make money. You are doing something new. New things take time, the argument goes. In fact, you are doing lots of new things. Your product may be new. Your business is. Running a business is new to you, too. It takes time to get the product right. It takes time for people to become aware of your business. They need to trust your brand before they will buy. They need to see that others are buying before they will. And you need to work out what you are doing. All of these very valid points create a perception that it's ok for your start-up to take time to make money.

Some start-ups need people to change behaviour. It takes time to persuade people they are wrong. It takes sustained effort to convince them to try your solution. And once you have, you've got to find someone else to persuade.

Most start-ups need to build awareness. If you are selling to businesses, they will have timetables and budgets for buying things. Approach at the wrong point and you may be waiting a year for the process to start. Even if you are selling haircuts, it isn't much use to

the person who has just had their hair cut.
And you have to sustain their interest until the
next time they need a cut. These things take
time.

The marketing techniques available to start-
ups favour time over impact. Big budgets
aren't available. It's not about a big bang to
create sudden excitement. It's softer
marketing; developing a loyal customer base,
word of mouth recommendations, press
stories. That takes time to work.

But how much time? Your business plan
makes a prediction. You know your costs and
you've guessed your income. You know how
much money you've started with and how
long it will last. You expect the business to
spend more than it earns for the first period –
perhaps three to six months. But that's ok.
You've got the cash to cover it.

And that's fine – unless you're wrong. If the
income doesn't arrive, the costs mount up.
The increased losses shorten the time you
have left. It's become more urgent to earn
money just as you learn it's becoming less
likely. And missing targets has a compound

effect. It means less money to spend on getting new customers. It's harder to change direction. Your losses have become a noose.

That's an argument for expecting less income in the early months. For making sure you have enough cash to cover your early losses. But you don't know if it's enough cash because you don't know what will need to spend.

Your plan is predicated on the obvious costs: rent, production, wages and so on. It assumes that people want your product. It assumes you were absolutely right about the costs of production. And it assumes you were right that your marketing would have the expected return. That's a lot of assumptions, requiring a lot of luck.

So you've already planned to make losses in the first months. And now you've discovered that you need even more cash before anyone is going to want the product. But you've already raised your start-up capital. Your backers knew they were taking a risk and now you've proved to them that you were wrong. Life has just become a lot harder.

If you plan to take a long time before getting customers, you will. That may be the sort of pop psychology to which this book is so opposed. But the further you expect to be from customers in your first month, the further you will be from customers. It's easy to expect it to take time to get customers. It creates a comfortable environment. But the easy decisions always cost the most.

Many companies wait too long before being 'open for business.' They are run by perfectionists who want to make sure they are 'ready' for customers. They worry about what they'll do if they get *too many* customers. They worry about how they'll recruit a Chief Financial Officer in nine months' time. They worry about how long it will take to break the US market. They launch on their terms.

This approach works only if you know that it will be alright in the end. It's a plan to hit and hope. It should be treated that way. Spending a year developing a product is justifiable if the product works at the end of the year. A three-month marketing plan is fine if the business flows at the end of three months.

Only sales validate your approach. You can develop the best possible product. You can devise the best marketing slogan. You can think of the best company logo. But they're only worth anything if a customer thinks so.

The process which delivers your first sale gives you something to repeat. It gives you something to grow. Before then, everything you are doing just might be totally wrong.

Isn't this all just about ensuring a return on investment (ROI)? Certainly the basics of business are important. The joy of a start-up is that you don't have to employ expensive accountants to calculate the ROI. The model is smaller and simpler. You know what you spend, how much it cost and what you were trying to achieve. That's a challenge for large, established businesses.

But ROI is too simplistic for a start-up. An investment suggests a level of certainty – or at least expectation. You are doing something that could reasonably be expected to work. A start-up doesn't have a reasonable expectation. It has a hunch. You need to find out whether anyone wants your product before you can expect an investment to deliver a return.

Investments also allow losses. A large company can afford to invest £1m in marketing, assuming that half will not generate a return. That's ok as long as the other half does. If a start-up invests £10,000 in marketing, however, everything has to work. There is no other half left to perform.

ROI also lacks urgency. An advert can build awareness whilst an email campaign can generate web hits. Over six to nine months, it might produce a 30% improvement in performance for a larger company. Meanwhile, over in start-up land, you've gone out of business, updated your LinkedIn profile and signed on for Jobseeker's Allowance.

So you need customers, as soon as possible. Customers bring permission. The permission to ask people what they liked and why. The permission to find out why they bought it. The permission to find out whether they'd recommend it Talking to a customer is no longer marketing. It's about building a relationship. It doesn't feel so uncomfortable.

Time is no healer. It's a corrosive agent. It gets in the way of customers. It replaces knowledge with supposition, certainty with assumptions, cash with debt. The longer things take, the worse they get. Even if success does arrive, it is worth less because it has come at a higher price.

Newscounter had all the time in the world. This was a business that spent two years in gestation. Two years when we should have been running the service at no cost. Two years in which we could have found out that there wasn't a business (or even a charity) in the idea, got over it and moved on to something else.

The nine months we spent 'running the business' weren't much better. We did things to get us closer to having customers. We simplified the pitch, redesigned the website, improved the service and removed the charges. They didn't work and we carried on. On enough occasions, we felt like as though we were making progress. But it wasn't progress towards a customer.

The successful start-ups were in a hurry. They didn't have years to spend assembling business plans. They wanted to get trading. Becky at Bare Conductive put it most memorably: 'whether succeed or fail, we wanted to do so quickly.' Alistair didn't quit his job until Grapple's first sale was in place. Andi and Perry were frustrated by how long it took to fit-out Blue Tit's salon – and they didn't even wait for the phone line to be installed!

#7 Copycats succeed quicker

Everyone says you need a USP. But how many businesses can you think of that actually have a unique selling point? For every Ryanair, there's an easyJet. For every Google, there's a Bing. Different, not unique.

Many founders think they are creating a new market. Not just a USP but a whole new way of doing business. It is doing something so totally new that there aren't any customers. There are no competitors, either. There's just an infinite pool of possibilities. And sooner or later, the idea will catch and spread.

For them, starting a business isn't the achievement. It's doing something amazing, something that makes you stand out, something that makes people talk. With a killer idea, your marketing is done for you. Without it, you are just another salesman.

It's not just about being a different colour, 10p cheaper or 12% more effective. Your product needs to be exceptional. You need to disrupt a market. If you aren't the next Facebook, a Google killer or an industry disrupter, I don't even want to know you. Another newsagent won't cure climate change.

Different is exciting. It's got 'talkability', buzz. People want to know. You don't have any competitors. There's a whole set of customers waiting just because it's new. New does the hard work. It grabs attention. New validates the product. New establishes the price.

We had to be bold. We had to be new. We had little to learn. The market would come to us. It would take time – but we had time. It would take money – and we had money. It would need interest – but new would create interest. It would need to work – but interest would make it work.

Perhaps. Maybe in Silicon Valley. But in the real world, new is suspicious. New is untested. New is confusing. I don't know what to do with new. What if it doesn't work? New threatens too many. New 'flashes', but it doesn't stick.

Forget Facebook. Forget Google. Forget Skype. They are not model start-ups. They are freaks. New is an awful starting point for entrepreneurs. New provides no set of expectations, no benchmark. There is no place to sell and no customers waiting to buy. There's no price. No money waiting to change hands. It might take six weeks, six months or six years – or never. New ideas need to work without income. New ideas need to survive without cash.

An innovative business needs to be a business to be innovative. Time is a luxury, income essential. The more cash you raise from investors, the greater the need for income.

The sooner the income arrives, the more time you have. But that's just a convenient sideshow. Customers validate innovation.

New means nothing if it doesn't catch on. You aren't hailed as a guru you are dismissed as a geezer.

Newscounter was obsessed with different. We had little to learn. We were right and needed to prove it. We forgot income. The longer we held on, the closer we would get to being proved right.

But no one thanked me for it. No one said goodbye when the company vanished. No one missed us when we were gone. Not even a flash in the pan.

If you are obsessed with innovation you're not starting a business, you are just playing a game. Stop, and be serious. You need to find the box your customer will put you in and get in. Once you're in that box, you need to look similar to the other balls in that box. You can be a different shade or a slightly different shape. But if the box is full of marbles, don't be a conker.

Grapple Mobile was innovative. They used an existing technology to build mobile applications for lots of different handsets more quickly. But it wasn't unique. They didn't invent mobile apps. They had an edge over the competition – a reason for customers to choose them – but it was at the margins. Bim's Kitchen wasn't the first sellers of cooking sauces – or indeed the first sellers of sauces for new cultural cuisines. Until James specialised in African sauces there was nothing unique about the offer. Blue Tit wasn't the first hairdresser on its own patch. Its trendy vibe wasn't unique for London – but they brought the two together in the same place at the right time.

Your start-up needs to be successful. If it makes something new – and succeeds – that's wonderful and truly rewarding. But if it fails, the invention has been discredited. It really is better first to achieve an obtainable goal than to fail reaching a dream.

#8 Nimble businesses lack purpose

Newscounter was always two steps away from a customer. We just had to fix that, and then do the other thing – then we could pitch to a customer. We weren't alone. A zombie start-up always needs to do two things before it can contemplate asking for cash. They rarely get closer.

Businesses often start at a leisurely pace. It's a bit like getting married (assuming you are in the asking seat). You decide to ask the question. You save for a ring. You think your partner will say 'yes'. You wait for the right time to ask. She does say 'yes'. You plan a wedding for the next year. You find a venue, a date and build to the big day. Everything builds towards it.

There's a point after which there's no turning back (without a loss of face). But you only realise you've passed it, not that you've reached it. No matter how well you prepare, the last few days feel busy.

Starting a business can provide lots of chances to get used to the idea. Writing the plan, speaking to people, looking for the venue. There are some essential steps. But if you had to sell to a customer tomorrow, what would stop you?

You are a special one. You have the courage to start a business. You are decisive. You are a 'can do' person. You don't prevaricate, you don't waver. But these attributes are not absolutes. Lots of founders start businesses assuming they will 'just do it' but accepting it will take months, if not years.

In 18 months we created 22 versions of the business plan 35 versions of the costs. We held 18 meetings with prospective investors and our little project team spoke at least weekly. We learnt nothing useful. Nothing we did changed anything we were planning to do. The basic model remained intact. Our certainties were strengthened. We were in a bubble, at a safe distance from customers.

We weren't ready for launch. We needed the website, for starters. We needed the board of directors to show we were impartial. We needed the price. We needed the logo and the good design. The time to maintain the website. It had to be a full-time pursuit.

We were preparing for a future that wouldn't exist. Our preparation was faultless but fruitless. You never truly know what will happen until you unveil your product. It happens to the best of them. Coca-Cola spent £1bn on the launch of New Coke. It failed. They got it wrong despite their cash, expertise and brand power. What makes you think that your piddling little start-up will be any different?

Working towards a launch is futile. There's too much you don't know. Think small. You choose a day for launch. You don't know what your customers are doing that day. You like the colour of your shop. Your customers don't. Think big: you pick a price. You don't know your competitor routinely discounts 25% from their advertised price. It gets worse: the more detailed your plan, the more you will be surprised by what you learn and the harder it will be to adapt.

Waiting to launch means missed opportunities. Every week that goes past is an opportunity to existing competitors to build on what they know. And they already know more than you. They are learning from customers, observing how they use the product. You aren't. Existing businesses are in the marketplace, crafting new adverts, measuring responses, re-targeting. You aren't. Other founders are at networking events, speaking at conferences, building their brand. You haven't yet told your boss. You can't measure those lost opportunities.

Your business starts before you know. It's not the launch day. It's not when you quit your job. It's the moment you pay the first bill. Your balance sheet is showing red. You are bleeding. Fail to fix it and you will eventually fail. The longer you lose money, the harder it will be to make money.

Get close to customers as soon as you can. Stay there. Spend as little as possible until a potential customer says you need to. Don't assume what they want. Never be more than a step away from meeting a customer. If you find a real barrier to a customer – they expect to see a website, for example – remove it.

#9 Think inside the box

Thinking inside the box is wildly unpopular. In fact, so few people do it that some don't feel a need to say that they're thinking outside the box any more. The box is *so* last century. It's now out of shot. Dead.

Starting a business is inherently creative. You spot an opportunity that no one else has spotted. You find new ways to do marketing on the cheap. You bring new products to new people. You are the darling of the consumer, showing what's possible. Start-ups aren't even aware of a box. They are breaking the mould. Disrupting tradition. Breaking down traditional orthodoxies. Turning old business models on their head. It's creative destruction, on steroids.

Founders are deeply creative. Whether finding new opportunities to make money, designing a product or just choosing a business name. You can't usually afford to buy it in, so you have to do it yourself. Founders aren't the sort of people to be deferential, bound by tradition. You don't favour business as usual. Whether it's Steve Jobs' black T-shirt or Richard Branson's unchanging mane, the iconic business founders do things differently. Creativity isn't just about the wild and wacky. It's about taking a new approach to old problems, seeing things differently and being willing to break things.

Books about start-ups love the pivot. The moment the founder looked at the business, worked out what was wrong and turned it into something else. The landfill provider that became a renewable energy provider.

The website design business that became social media strategists, and so on.

So what would you do differently if you knew that thinking inside the box might save your start-up? Creativity has its limits. Past performance sets an expectation for future performance. Tried and tested isn't dull, it's predictable. It's what you know that's important, not what you don't know.

Let me explain.

Thinking inside the box is most important when your business isn't working. That's the moment when creativity feels most important. Everything you thought you knew has been proven wrong. You don't have any good reason to trust your judgment. Your confidence is low. You are tired. And that's when panic sets in. That's when you are most vulnerable. You don't have much time. You can't afford more mistakes.

Yet because you are nothing, you could be anything. The further away from your current circumstances, the more plausible it seems. You can put right all of your mistakes. You can clearly see why this is such a good idea when that was such a bad idea. If you can only start afresh, you will build a successful business.

Expertise builds businesses. You develop expertise by knowing more about your specialist area. If you've spent months learning about how men in your town eat cupcakes, that's your specialist area. You may dream of being a dog-groomer 200 miles away. But you are Mr Cupcake. You will find success by learning more about that. A fresh start is also a blank canvas.

When Newscounter failed, the world was my oyster. We were in the business of correcting inaccurate reports. So we could develop a widget for people's web browsers that would flash with a correction every time they visited a disputed web page. Or we could run a weekly TV debate between journalists and business people discussing the merits of a story. Or maybe even an online satirical magazine mocking the mistakes in the mainstream media. I wasn't an expert. I was no more likely to run a successful TV show than I had in running a website. What I did wasn't valuable. I had found nothing to sell.

The successful entrepreneurs were all experts in their fields. Hairdressing, mobile sales, cooking sauces and conductive paint. It wasn't by chance that those entrepreneurs set up those businesses. They certainly couldn't have started each other's business. It didn't leave them short of creative options. But nor were they swamped with myriad mirages.

James Adedeji didn't stop cooking sauces and start importing African food. He didn't even take the popularity of his sauces as permission to pursue his idea of running a restaurant. He thought inside the box. He made good sauces and wanted to sell more good sauces. To do that they needed to be distinctive. Alistair Crane discovered that his entire business model was flawed. People wanted apps, not a software licence to build apps. He didn't find an alternative application for his software. He didn't abandon the software and start again designing mobile applications.

The successful start-ups thought inside the box. They used their expertise. They studied the market. They looked deep within themselves. And they tweaked their businesses to better appeal to the market.

#10 Accumulate to speculate

The start-up often begins with a big bill. A product that someone else has to make. Without that product, you can't sell anything to customers. So you raise money, sell equity – or both. Then the product gets built. And the customer doesn't want it. A product, no money and no prospects.

Maybe we just need some cash for marketing. If only we had a good website. Perhaps a really good introductory video. Or just a sales person. If we paid to attend a conference, we'd meet all our potential customers. We just need a bit more money.

You spend some more cash. Ok, so we've found out why that didn't work. Let's redesign the website. The business name didn't catch on. Our product description wasn't understood. We'll fix those with the remaining cash and take it back to customers.

And on, and on, and on.

We've got a great opportunity. It's a really hot lead. It's a massive customer and they've shown interest. We need to really impress them at the meeting. Let's personalise the widget. Let's give them a free trial. Let's take them out to lunch.

The costs never come down. The income gets as close as a mirage. But this business inhabits the land of the undead. It just needs more cash.

We were aiming too small. We should have been thinking globally. The current investors had taken us as far as they could, so what we really needed from the next round of fundraising is contacts. Someone who really understood the vision. Someone who had been there and done it. Someone who could mentor us.

The balance sheet began red. It didn't get better. We weren't alone.

So many businesses are always holding out for the next development. Never cutting costs because they're on the cusp of a breakthrough, never breaking even because they're too big for their boots. There's just never enough cash.

Start-ups without enough cash also have too much cash. They've been cautious but never abstemious. Spend doesn't generate a return because it hasn't had to. Money has been spent on theories and hunches rather than essentials. The business doesn't know what's essential because it's always had something.

Entrepreneurs with too much cash buy things *they* need, not what their customers ask for. They are more worried about minimising mistakes than maximising what's right. They second-guess the customer and anticipate the market. They are in for a penny, in for a pound. It's immodest, presumptuous and inherently risky.

The alternative is making cash. Starting small, selling something for a profit. Investing that money to sell something else. Not walking in to the den and asking investors for £100,000 for a 10% stake in an idea. But building a brand, gaining experience and developing a business.

Newscounter had spent almost £30,000 before day 0.

And we truly believed there was no alternative. We had to get the right name. We must not break the law on copyright. The product and the website had to contain all the relevant features: they were mutually dependent. That demanded an expensive level of sophistication. Once we started, there was my salary and attendant costs.

None of the successful start-ups profiled here has costs as high as Newscounter. Ok, so Grapple had spent the best part of £1m. But that was an asset. Revenue brought costs. Bare Conductive needed to put in a large order for its first batch of paint. Bim's Kitchen needed to buy ingredients and jars to meet its large order. But these were done in the knowledge that revenue was forthcoming, not just as an aspiration but as a clear 'it's going to happen in 60 days' expectation.

Revenue before costs creates value. You've now got a business. It might not be enough to persuade a high street bank to give a loan, but an investor might. And you aren't offering

50% of your idea for £500,000 either. You can look Aunty Barbara in the eye when she asks if she'll get her money back.

Better still, you might not need investment. You might have enough income to invest your own cash. And like Andi and Perry, you'll take a much harder look at the return it's going to generate. When you begin your business with costs and no immediate expectation of return, it puts you in the wrong mentality. You've already the curse of the marketing department – you'd cut half your costs if only you knew which half to cut.

#11 Good enough is good enough

It's better to be surprised how much you can achieve with so little than how much it takes to achieve so little. The former is cheap. The latter is heart-breaking. If you can get a customer on the basis of a personalised email, it's cost you almost nothing. You can spend more to get more. But if your first customer comes from a £10,000 billboard advert, you'll have no way of knowing whether a phone call would have sufficed.

Keeping costs down is important. If you can avoid taking a wage from the business before it's generating income you'll give yourself a much higher chance of success. And there's no point in not taking a salary if you are just paying someone else's salary. Employing people brings certainty of cost. It should be avoided until you've certainty of income.

Marketing costs are also ripe for pruning. That may run counter to accepted logic. But the more you achieve with less, the better. But there are costs that don't make start-ups blink. Entrepreneurs buy logos, expensive website design and pay for legal costs without any chance of revenue within the next four weeks. If you can get a customer through personal relationships at no cost – great. It may not be something you can repeat at scale. But it's revenue, it's a start. The cash can be used to improve the logo or produce a nice homepage to the website. And the more customers you attract, and the earlier they purchase, the better you will understand whether you really need to spend £3,000 on a website.

You don't launch a business on a whim. It isn't some career break, midlife crisis or flight of fancy. It's a big, profound and wrenching experience. It takes more of your time than anything you've ever done before. It costs more money than anything you've ever spent before (save your house, possibly). And it does more to influence the direction of your career than anything else.

There's a temptation to make long term decisions. Your business plan discusses a three year exit strategy. If you are serious about it, then you need to be looking long term. This isn't about getting through the first six months but building a business that can scale. You want to demonstrate that it can scale. That's not just about delivering a sale to one person, or even just breaking-even. It's about building a company with realistic and exciting growth prospects. Who wants to be a corner shop when you could be building Google?

But to last, you must first breathe. Anything which puts that at risk can suffocate your business. There's no more bitter people than the founders who failed because a single deal fell apart. (Some of these are also Everton fans.)

It feels petty to look short-term. If you think small, it may end up costing more money than necessary. And no one wants to waste money. If you are printing 250 business cards, you might as well get 500. You don't want a website that's going to crash as soon as you get your first feature piece in a national magazine. When you hire your first employee, you won't have time to restructure all your computer systems, things will be too busy.

The decisions you cannot undo are those which cost you money. The more money you spend, the less flexibility you have. You need to be as flexible as possible for as long as possible. With this in mind, you don't make decisions that are right or wrong. Your decisions need only to be right for now. You can be wrong, but not for long.

When I was growing up, there were two big computer games: Sonic the Hedgehog and Super Mario Brothers. No one had mastered the games. I'm not certain that they could be 'won' (for commercial reasons, they couldn't be lost, either). The gamer's objective was to get to the next level.

It would invariably be harder, quicker and have bigger pitfalls. But once you had the passcode, you could access the next level. The best gamer in the class was not the gamer who had won the game but the one who was on the highest level.

Your start-up faces the Sonic challenge. You need to find out how to reach the next level. Everything you do needs to be pointed in that direction. The only meaningful preparation is to be found in efficient completion of the current level. That level might be delivering your first sale, delivering enough sales to break-even or enough repeat business to know your cost-base is covered each month. Until you get there, you have no idea of the challenges that are in store.

So what does it mean to have total devotion to your level? Making decisions that are right for now. When you hire staff, hire the skills you need now – not the skills for six months' time if the business continues to grow. If you are buying a service, don't buy one in the hope that you'll grow into it. Buy one that meets your needs today. If you are renting equipment, get something that fits your business, not the business you want to be.

If everything goes well, you have to go back to someone. You'll say 'Bad news, I've got more money than expected. Can I give you some more in exchange or a bigger service?'

Possibly embarrassing. But not exactly a deal-breaker. And believe me, infinitely preferable to the alternative conversation: 'My business wasn't as successful as I hoped. Can we give you less money, please?' You just look foolish.

We made numerous mistakes in this regard. None of them were business killers in themselves but when combined they represented a significant cost to the business. And they showed that my attitude was wrong. Newscounter bought a 12-month web hosting package that would have been robust if we'd had 1,000 times the number of website users. It cost as much to host, with our few hundred visitors per day accessing kilobytes of data as our social media monitoring software cost with gigabytes of data daily and a similar number of visitors. We bought an email service that could distribute a mailing list to thousands of subscribers. It dodged spam filters and measured the number of clicks on each link in the email. That would have been valuable data and a significant labour-saving device. If only someone wanted to receive the email. It was inefficient to use it to email 20 friends.

You'll last if you live to breathe. Aim for the next step. Income increases value. Cash can fix problems. Value attracts investment. Reach the next stage and revel in the new problems facing your business. It's short-term and it's tactical.

But it'll keep you alive. Who knows what the next level will bring?

Blue Tit opened without a phone line. Grapple delivered its first sale without a website. Bare Conductive had an order from Sony before the founders agreed to start a business. Each added more value. Blue Tit's phone line brought in customers. Its website brought in more. Grapple's website generated leads and its PR got the company on pitch lists. But there were plenty of things they didn't do. They didn't invest in expensive banners to do press photos. Remember that Alistair stuck a company logo, printed in the office, behind his head to do a conference call with a business website.

By starting with nothing, each successful start-up could learn what they really needed to do to add value. And if it wasn't, they didn't do it. There were no vanity trimmings, no long-term investments in the hope of a yield in six months' time, but there was a sharp focus on the present and a clear head for the future.

#12 It's not about the money
The scars of Newscounter meant that I was desperate for income at any price. Trufflenet brought instant success. We were away. We had a customer as soon as the software was ready and our income targets in sight within the first three months. Surely we were on the path to success?

Business isn't just about earning money. It isn't that simple. It has to be repeatable and scalable. There needs to be a process. Without a proven process there's little real value in the business. The value remains in your head.

Trufflenet's success had been neither. I was so obsessed with income I couldn't believe it wouldn't be enough. And because I didn't realise, I didn't know where to turn. Our first customer was an old contact that I hadn't met in two years. The second was a friend of the company secretary. We couldn't repeat either. The money wasn't unhelpful but it didn't give any clues to what would work and what wouldn't.

Self-employed people don't have a process. They sell their time and there's plenty of honour in that. But it's not a business. There's a limit to how much time they can sell. When they aren't doing, they aren't earning. And when they are doing they aren't selling. They are the value and it walks out at closing time. If they get run over by a bus, so does the business.

Creating value demands creating a process. That's a killer for the creative entrepreneur.

Process is dull. It smacks of bureaucracy. But the process is your bible. It's your way of surviving. It's the first evidence that the business is more than you doing what you do.

A business process gets new customers. It finds out how much marketing you have to do to get a customer. How many customers will return and how often. It determines what the customers will get and how they'll get it. The process is a sequence events with various inputs and outputs. If we send 50 flyers, five will return the form and one will become a customer. Therefore, if we send twice as many flyers next time we expect two customers.

The business process trains new staff. You don't need to search for an all-round genius just like you. Just someone who can follow instruction. And if the instruction appears to break, or an alternative emerges, it can be challenged and the process updated.

Some business have obvious processes. Bim's Kitchen had recipes for its sauces. Actually, it didn't to begin with. James made it up as he went along. The recipes had to be written down for the sauces to be sold in shops – and pass tests set by the Food Standards Agency. As soon as they were codified, the business was no longer dependent on James.

But there were other, subtle parts to the process. The decision to have taster pots at the market stall to attract customers, for example. That the logos still felt like the sauces were handmade. The ingredients printed in bigger typeface than you'd see on a supermarket jar.

Blue Tit had a recipe too. It wasn't just recruiting like-minded, similarly talented hairdressers. The model that supported the first salon was used for the second and third. Andi and Perry chose Clapton for the second salon because it had the 'up and coming' features of Dalston along with low rent. They prevaricated over the third salon to wait for the right area of London at the right rental price.

These processes are based on lessons the business learnt: some deliberate, some unwitting. But they are critical to the success of each. Income alone wouldn't cut it.

#13 Hard work can kill

' "How was your day?" is a question that matters a lot more than it seems. '
Tribes (Seth Godin, Piatkus, 2008)

No one created a great business without hard work. Founders are driven people. They do it with passion. It consumes their life. They don't arrive at work at 9am and then eat their breakfast; they don't leave at 5.30pm. They don't combine multiple interests. They know one thing very well. It's all they want to do. It's all they *do* do.

Because successful founders work hard, you must work hard to be successful. That's true of anyone who excels in their field. David Beckham stayed on after training to practise free kicks. Pep Guardiola is an obsessive football manager. Margaret Thatcher existed on a few hours' sleep a night, by all accounts.

You set up a business knowing that it would be like this. You want it to be like this. You like being under pressure. It's how you perform best. It's only when you are really feeling the heat that you get fully engaged. Pressure and deadlines get you motivated like few other people you know. It brings out the best in you; it makes you feel alive.

You want to stretch yourself further than you have ever been before. You want to find that you can achieve more than you expect. You know it won't be easy but you've never shirked a challenge. You want to find out more about yourself. You think you can do this but you want to prove it to the non-believers.

Win or lose, you want to know that you've given it everything you have got. Your personal life is going to be on hold until you've got this sorted.

In fact, you know that you've got little prospect of a personal life. That will come later, when you have been successful. But it's not just about your time. You will do *anything* to make this work. No sacrifice is too great. That will make the story of heroism all the more compelling when you do succeed. Every penny you have will go towards this moment.

But life isn't fair. Working hard *isn't* enough. You have to be doing the right thing. Practising the wrong thing over and over again makes it less likely you will do the right thing. The most important thing you do won't take very long at all. Selling to a customer might take as much as an hour. You may even need to meet twice. But there are all sorts of hours when you can't sell. The bits in between are critically important, but must they all be filled with work?

What if long hours made your success less likely? There ought to be little room for doubt. Setting up a business isn't a race to see who can be first to complete a pre-defined list of tasks. It isn't (usually) about selling as much product as you can before the sun goes down (thanks to 'The Apprentice'). Starting a business is about creating something. That needs creativity. Creativity can come in the middle of the night. But not if you've been working all day. Scientists believe that when you move on to do different tasks your brain can process problems differently. You are more likely to come up with that 'brainwave' moment if you exercise, read a book or listen to music than if you continue to plug away at the same problem, minute after minute.

But how can that be true? Successful people all work long hours. As do gamblers. In fact, most people say they work long hours. Many do. It doesn't make you successful.

You do not need to psych yourself up to run a start-up. If you did, you would not have got this far. There is no need artificially to pressure yourself. There is enough that comes with running a start-up.

It's hardest to control your hours in the first few weeks of a start-up. You've made the decision to go for it. You know how far you are from being a successful business. And if you've recently quit your job, you have an alarming amount of free time. It's disconcerting enough to be doing something new. You don't want to add to it by watching the lunchtime news. But this is when you need the most creativity. And you need to be most comfortable at needing to discover new things.

Don't pretend to know what you should be doing.

That's a shortcut to producing endless strategy documents. To changing numbers on a spreadsheet for the sake of it, to setting up structures and processes that will never work in practice because practice will be so far removed from your imagination. So embrace the time. Rest, learn, discover.

Very quickly pressure comes from all sorts of sources, some of which will surprise you have others that won't. The staff put pressure on you: the pressure to deploy them in a constructive manner; the pressure to elevate their careers; the pressure to help them succeed and fulfil their potential; the pressure to earn enough money to pay their wages. The investors also put pressure on you: the pressure to meet the targets that were set; the pressure to exceed them; the pressure to do even better than you were previously. Customers are another sort of pressure. They need work done by a certain date. You've assumed that it needs to be done to a particular standard. They want you to meet them at a time of their choosing. If they choose to alter their requirements, they will pressure you to accept this. They put pressure on you through the timescale and budget that they set.

You can't stop your mind reinforcing this pressure. You want to do well in new business meetings.

You want to impress your prospects, clients and investors. You want to prove that you can do it and that you are uniquely placed to do this well. You want credibility amongst your peers and admiration from your friends. You want to be able to look them in the eye and tell them how well you are doing.

Most importantly, you want to succeed. Whether you are succeeding for children, family, yourself – or just that school teacher who wrote you off. Each setback increases the intensity and pressure on you to finally prevail.

You may react well to pressure. And you may have experience of dealing with pressure in the past. But I'd be amazed if you had ever experienced the unremitting, unrelenting pressure of a start-up. It never leaves you. Previously you may have taken your work home and even had an important job. But it was contained. You were part of a wider game. Even on your days off as a start-up your mind is on the job. Fail and it has profound consequences for your personal life.

There are, therefore, some things that you do not need to do to increase the pressure. As far as possible – if it is at all – you need to depersonalise the success of the business. It isn't about you, it's about the product. It isn't about you, it's about the team.

It isn't about you, it's about the market place. You will make mistakes and you will do some things that others would have done differently. But you did these for sensible reasons and made decisions that others would have made in your position. And colleagues didn't exactly stand in your way.

You are already gambling your career and income prospects by starting up a business. Throwing your mortgage, life savings or pension into the pot is not going to make the bet any safer but it might make it so sensitive that you increase the likelihood of failing.

Some people work long hours. Some say they do. Others suffer from presenteeism – appearing to work long hours by sitting at the desk whilst fiddling, working unproductively. At Newscounter, I really did.

Speed mattered. If a misleading story went uncorrected for more than half a day, it would be too late. The web is all about speed. Rolling news bulletins, articles updated on websites. The sooner an organisation could use our service to correct a story the greater the impact we would have.

Before we launched the business we did two dummy runs. The first took over three hours. It was so tedious it was hard to concentrate. The second took two and a half hours.

The lack of a deadline meant that it wasn't a true exercise. But at least we had some expectation. We didn't yet have a website so we couldn't know how long it would take to publish the stories – but we imagine it wouldn't be considerable.

In my first week, I woke up at 2am to collect the daily newspaper delivery. I read each page of each paper and marked the stories of interest for the website. That took two hours. I then went back to bed until 8m before waking up to write up the stories and begin contacting the organisations involved. In total I was sleeping five hours a night. But the broken sleep was a disaster. I had a heavy cold by the weekend.

The following week I woke at 3.30am to begin the day. Reading the newspapers still took two hours but then I continued the process: writing up the stories and emailing the organisations involved. I was still getting five hours sleep but the continuity helped immeasurably. I'd have a shower mid-morning, after one round of contacting organisations. The rest of the day was spent doing various ad hoc tasks.

I knew that I was tired. I now know that the broken sleep that accompanies the arrival of young babies made me less tired than doing that job. But I didn't know how tired I was. Three changes gave me some signals. I'd forget things. I'd go to the kitchen and forget why I had gone. I'd leave the bus and panic that I'd left my bag. I became anxious. Looking out of a bus window I'd be terrified that I was about to witness a crash. I'd assume that the motorbike or pedestrian was about to be knocked over. I'd have to grip the seat and look away. And then I'd have the repetitive dream of watching a plane fall from the sky.

When you're sleeping five hours a night for months on end, you can do without bad dreams.

The process was pointless. In a year no one was able to give us a response before midday. Our customers weren't equipped to respond that quickly. Our web visitors weren't more likely to come to the website at 9am than 11am. Speed mattered only to the business plan.

I met people with good ideas. Why don't you build a widget? What about dissecting one story a day? What about a weekly podcast? Why don't you interview the people involved in the story? What about a league table of the newspapers and brands? All good ideas, all worth trying. I wasn't capable. Enough energy to sleepwalk through a process. None left to create a business.

I have no idea of the personal sacrifices made by the investors in my business. If I did, perhaps I would not live with the guilt that would ensue.

I am delighted, though, that I never got close to touching our mortgage (we have no other meaningful assets). It never even crossed my mind. If it had, we would have crossed a Rubicon. And I would be regretting it deeply.

I did lose income that I could have earned elsewhere. I did go months without any income at all. And through it all I depended on my wife to continue paying the bills. That was hard enough, and remains difficult for us. I am only pleased that it wasn't a great deal worse.

I have seen people that have lost it all. There's nothing that you can do but cry with them. I have seen people on the road to losing it all and that is deeply painful. I recently met a man establishing something that he was madly in love with but I knew would not succeed. His life savings, built up through a successful career, were being invested in this venture. He knew too little of the sector. There was little I could do – but I hope that I can do more in the future. It remains the most important service performed by on 'Dragons' Den': when the dragons tell an inventor that he or she should quit.

So spend time away from the business. Don't get too embroiled in the detail. Take a step back and try, as hard as you might, to be objective. Do something else. Experience new things.

Read a book, experience art or just go to sleep. And don't expect immediate results. If your costs are low, you can do it. If your business is struggling, few will notice. And you might just identify the path to salvation.

Conclusion

Barclays used to run a TV advert that appealed to entrepreneurs. It showed two people arriving at an office for a meeting. One person played the role of receptionist, office cleaner, PA and company CEO. It was a neat way of demonstrating the 'jack of all trades' nature of running a small business.

But starting a business isn't just about doing lots of different roles in your business. It's not even about being an expert at one, and passable at many others. You have two totally different tasks. First, to learn how to run your business – and all of its parts. Second, to learn how to run a start-up, with all of its requirements.

An entrepreneur is taking on two roles with many functions, working for (unfortunately) no money and working (not quite) every hour of every day. Their Mum won't understand what they do. Their friends won't swoon at their feet. Their partner will be fidgety and anxious that their future is also on the line.

The pay-off is uncertain. You might make enough to sustain your lifestyle.

You may sell the business and make a dent in your mortgage. But there's also faint chance that you might change the course of your life – and that of your children. And maybe their children. And those plaudits will be well-deserved.

It's never been cheaper or easier to start a business. Full-time employment has never been less secure. Many people yearn for the opportunity to pursue different interests and heaven knows that the country needs more successful businesses.

If you do it, do it well. Tell others how you did it. And help guide others away from the pitfalls. It's your duty.

Index

Printed in Great Britain
by Amazon.co.uk, Ltd.,
Marston Gate.